ANCIENT ROMANS

AND THEIR

NEIGHBORS

AN ACTIVITY GUIDE

SIMONETTA CARR

CHICAGO REVIEW PRESS

Published by Chicago Review Press Incorporated
814 North Franklin Street
Chicago, Illinois 60610
ISBN 978-0-914091-71-4

Library of Congress Cataloging-in-Publication Data
Is available from the Library of Congress.

Cover and interior design: Sarah Olson
Cover images: (*front*) Etruscan jug in bucchero,
William Randolph Hearst Collection, Los Angeles
County Museum of Art; Celtic sword, Rogers Fund,
1999, Metropolitan Museum of Art, NY; Carthaginian
glass pendant, gift of J. Pierpont Morgan, 1917, to the
Metropolitan Museum of Art, NY; Emperor Augustus
as Pontifex Maximus, ©Art Resource; Gold torque, gift
of J. Pierpont Morgan, George Blumenthal, and Fletcher
Fund, 2005, to the Metropolitan Museum of Art, NY;
Roman Colosseum, Noppasin Wongchum/Shutterstock;
(*back*) Carthaginian statuette of a tambourine player,
©Art Resource; Etruscan handle in the shape of an
animal, The Walters Art Museum

Illustrations: Lindsey Cleworth Schauer
Map design: Chris Erichsen

Printed in the United States of America
5 4 3 2 1

CONTENTS

 # PART I: THE ROMANS • 1

PART IV: THE CARTHAGINIANS · 107

INTRODUCTION

The ancient Romans lived hundreds of years ago, but their influence is still around us—in our language, our buildings, our laws, our ideas of liberty and citizenship, and much more. They still excite us in action movies and video games, and some of our common expressions relate to Roman history. This book will help you to recognize these enduring signs of Rome in your daily life. You'll learn about Rome's fascinating history, from its legendary birth to its unexpected end, and see how it survived both foreign attacks and devastating civil wars to become one of the greatest **empires** in history, influencing and absorbing dozens of different cultures.

In our imagination, Romans were strong, powerful, and brave. They lived in luxurious mansions and conquered the rest of the world with their strong armies. But that is not a full picture of their lives. They had humble beginnings and learned much from their neighbors. Scholars believe their willingness to learn from other nations and to respect their cultures played a great role in Rome's success.

Today, these neighbors are not equally well known, but they are fascinating and important. The Etruscans, inhabitants of modern-day Tuscany, created a unique, colorful, and highly refined culture, pioneering many architectural elements that have been attributed to the Romans. The Celts, with their fascinating history of druids and magic potions, were a complex and resourceful population that left important marks across Europe. The Carthaginians are remembered most for Hannibal's daring crossing of the Alps with African elephants, but there is much more to their history and culture. For a time, they were the most powerful force along the Mediterranean Sea.

Ancient Romans and Their Neighbors will give you a glimpse of the lives of these unique people. You will learn how they spent their days, what they ate, how they dressed, what gods they worshiped, how they governed, and how they fought. You will relive extraordinary events and moments from their everyday lives—how they created artwork, cooked meals, and overcame obstacles.

TIME LINE

This time line of the Romans and their neighbors ends with the fall of the Western Roman Empire, because the Eastern Empire, which continued for about 1,000 years longer, was different in many ways, and would require a book of its own.

	1200 BC	1100	1000	900	800	700	600	500

ROMANS

- c. 1200 BC Greek hero Aeneas lands in Italy
- c. 900 Early settlements in Rome
- 753 Foundation of Rome
- 753–509 Rome ruled by kings

Founding of the Roman Republic 509 •

ETRUSCANS

- c. 800 Beginning of the Etruscan civilization

CELTS

- 750 Celtic settlement at Hallstat, Austria

Celtic civilization develops at La Téne 500 •

CARTHAGINIANS

400	300	200	100 BC	1	100 AD	200	300	400	500 AD

• 197–133 Roman wars in Spain

• 117 Largest expansion of Roman Empire

• 88–83 First Roman Civil War

• 180 End of *Pax Romana*

• 264–241 First Punic War over Sicily

Diocletian reorganizes the Roman Empire 286 •

Second Roman Civil War 49 •

Constantine declares Christianity legal 313 •

• 44 Caesar is killed

Rome is sacked by Visigoths 410 •

Octavian defeats his opponents at Actium 31 •

Rome is sacked by Vandals 455 •

Octavian starts ruling as Augustus 27 •

End of the Western Roman Empire 476 •

• 80 Rome final takeover of Etruria

• 390 Celts attack Rome

• 121 Transalpine Gaul becomes a Roman province

Caesar's war against the Gauls 58–52 •

• 61 Boudicca's rebellion in Britain

• 298 Celts defeated by Greeks at Delphi

• 55 Caesar's expedition into Britain

• 278 Celts settle in Galatia

• 52 Gallic King Vercingetorix surrenders to Rome

• 225–220 Romans conquer Cisalpine Gaul

• 46 Vercingetorix is killed at Caesar's triumph

Emperor Claudius begins conquest of Britain 43 •

• 122 Hadrian's wall defends Roman northern borders

• 241–220 Carthaginian conquest of Spain

• 219–202 Second Punic War

• 149–146 Third Punic War; Carthage is destroyed

PART I: THE ROMANS

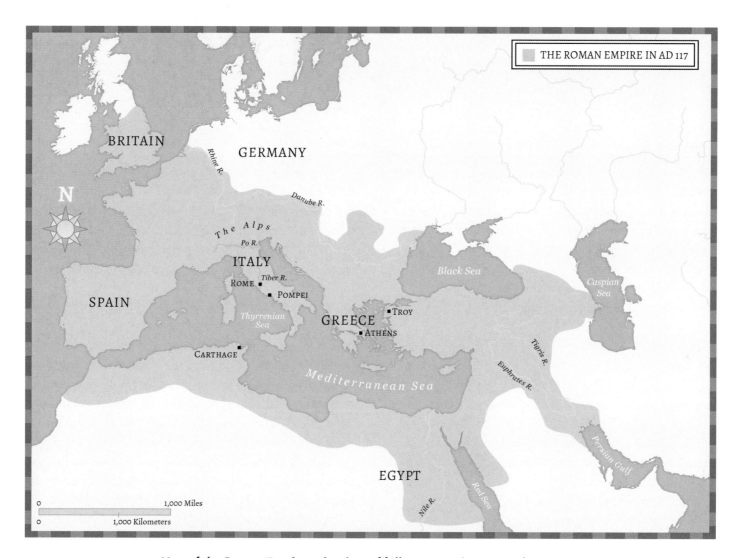

THE ROMAN EMPIRE IN AD 117

BRITAIN

GERMANY

Rhine R.

Danube R.

N

The Alps

Po R.

ITALY

Black Sea

Caspian Sea

ROME *Tiber R.*

POMPEI

SPAIN

Thyrrenian Sea

GREECE TROY

ATHENS

Tigris R.

CARTHAGE

Mediterranean Sea

Euphrates R.

Persian Gulf

EGYPT

Nile R. *Red Sea*

0 ———————— 1,000 Miles

0 ———————— 1,000 Kilometers

Map of the Roman Empire at its time of fullest expansion, around AD 117. It included 40 provinces spread over 2 million square miles.

ROMAN HISTORY

The small group of people who built their huts along the Tiber River couldn't have imagined they started one of the greatest civilizations the world has ever known. But they knew they had chosen a great location where food was easy to grow and sell thanks to the river and the nearby Tyrrhenian Sea.

Most historians agree that Rome began when local tribes banded together for safety and strength near where the Roman Forum stands today. Roman legends, however, are much more fun and colorful.

The Legends

The story of Romulus and Remus, told in many versions, is the most popular legend of Rome's founding. As told by the Roman historian Livy, it all started in the lost city of Alba Longa in the Alban Hills southeast of Rome, when a prince named Amulius grabbed the throne from his older brother, Numitor.

To eliminate challengers, Amulius killed Numitor's sons and forced Numitor's daughter, Sylvia, to become a priestess of Vesta, goddess of home and family. Priestesses of Vesta could not marry, so Amulius was confident she wouldn't have any children to one day claim their right to the throne. To his surprise, Sylvia gave birth to twins, claiming the father was the Roman god Mars.

Enraged, Amulius imprisoned Sylvia and ordered his men to drown the children in the Tiber. His men put them in a basket and placed it in the river, but the basket never sank. As the story goes, a female wolf heard the babies' cries, breast-fed them, and cared for them as if they were her own cubs. Finally, a shepherd named Faustulus saw them and took them to his home, raising them with his wife, Larentia.

When the boys grew up, they discovered who they were and what had happened to their grandfather. In revenge, they killed Amulius, returned the throne to Numitor, and left to found a new city.

After the city was built, the two brothers argued over who should be king. They asked the gods for a sign. Remus was the first to receive one: he saw six vultures in flight. To the ancients, this was a token of good news. Remus was still rejoicing when Romulus saw 12 vultures. Each man was declared king by his followers, one because he saw the birds first, the other because he saw twice as many. Eventually, the argument turned violent. Romulus killed Remus and seized the throne, and the city was named Rome in his honor. This story was immortalized in many images, and the wolf became the symbol of Rome.

It's hard to know how much of this is truth and how much is legend. However, this story dates the foundation of Rome as 753 BC, close to what **archaeologists** believe was Rome's beginning.

The Greeks gave a different account. Their story starts after the Trojan War, when a man named Aeneas escaped the burning city of Troy (in today's Turkey) carrying his aging father on his shoulders and leading his son by the hand. Aeneas finally settled in Italy, where his son founded a city. However, the Trojan War ended around 1200 BC, much earlier than the foundation of Rome. Some Roman historians combined the two legends, saying that Aeneas's son founded Alba Longa, where Romulus and Remus were born a few centuries later.

The Kings

According to legend, Rome had a total of seven consecutive kings, starting with Romulus. Historians think this number might be incorrect. If seven kings ruled from 753 to 509 BC, each king would have ruled roughly 35 years, which was uncommon in those days. There might have been more kings, or this **monarchy** may have lasted for a shorter period of time.

These early kings were different from modern kings. They were more like tribal chiefs, and the throne was not passed down from father to son. Each king was elected by the Senate, a group of influential citizens. Kings led their people in wars, approved laws, and were the link between their subjects and their gods.

To grow the city, Romulus invited everyone to come, including outlaws and runaway slaves. Since these were mostly men, he tried to convince surrounding nations to give them their women in marriage. Everyone refused. Romulus then invited these nearby nations to a great sporting event, and large crowds gathered. At a given signal, the unmarried men of Rome kidnapped the single foreign women and took them to their homes.

Romulus explained to the women that the young men had every intention of loving them and treating them well, and, according to the story, the women agreed to marry them and stay in Rome. The women's fathers, however, were angry and started a war against Rome. The women put an end to the conflict, pleading with the men not to kill each other. They didn't want to lose their husbands or their fathers.

Whether or not this story is true, from the beginning Rome was composed of people of different tribes and nations and grew quickly by granting citizenship to loyal allies and freed slaves. In fact, Rome's last three kings were Etruscan.

Republic, Expansion, and Civil War

The last king of Rome, Tarquinius Superbus ("the Proud"), imposed forced labor on the citizens and stole from neighboring nations to increase his glory. The Romans eventually became tired of the bullying behavior and, in 509, expelled him and his son. To prevent further abuses, they elected new leaders called **consuls** and declared Rome a **republic**, from the Latin *res publica*, meaning "public property."

Tarquinius fought to take back Rome, with the help of the Etruscan king, Porsenna, but they failed. The Romans later told stories of brave heroes from the battle, such as Horatio, who fought the Etruscans singlehandedly as his men destroyed a bridge behind him, preventing the enemy from advancing into Roman territory. Horatio then leapt into the Tiber in full armor and swam safely to the other side. Many outsiders tried to conquer Rome in the early years, and the Romans suffered many defeats. But they learned from them and became strong enough to take over the entire Italian peninsula, both by force and by offering citizenship and benefits to those who joined them willingly.

The general Julius Caesar made the greatest conquests outside of Italy, including Gaul (today's France), parts of Germany, and some of North Africa. He also explored Britain and opened the door for a full conquest of Egypt, which was a major supplier of wheat, **papyrus**, **linen**, and other important products.

Caesar became powerful and well loved by the people. The Roman Senate feared he might assume too much power and ordered him to disband his army. Caesar didn't think this was fair, and he knew that many who were asking him to step down were corrupt. In 49 BC, he took his army across the Roman border, starting a **civil war**.

The war was mostly fought in Greece. Caesar's main adversary, known as Pompey the Great, died in 48 BC, but Caesar continued to fight in northern Africa against Pompey's allies. He returned to Rome in 46 BC, where he was greeted with honors. By this time, the Senate had come to recognize his abilities and valor. They gave him increasing power until, in 44 BC, they proclaimed him **dictator** for life.

Some senators, however, were terribly worried. The position of dictator was legal and approved by the Senate in cases of extreme need, but only for six months. Having a dictator for life was like having an absolute king—something Romans had fought to avoid. It looked like the end of the republic they loved. Other senators thought Caesar was too generous to the poor, and they worried they could lose their property and status. Whatever their motives, a group of senators planned an attack.

On March 15, 44 BC, Caesar attended a meeting at the Senate, despite a warning from his wife, Calpurnia, who had had an ominous dream. When he arrived, the senators surrounded him, then stabbed him with **daggers** until he died.

The Empire

Caesar's murder shocked and divided the people of Rome and their allies. Most Romans were outraged, because Caesar had won the hearts of his people. Others took it as a positive step in restoring the republic.

Once again, a civil war started. Those who had supported Caesar were his longtime friend Marc Antony, his adopted son and heir Octavian, and a military commander named Marcus Lepidus. After working together to defeat Brutus and Cassius, two of Caesar's main assassins, Antony and Octavian started to fight each other. They eventually faced each other in a naval battle off the coast of Greece near a city named Actium, where Octavian won once and for all.

Octavian believed that Rome needed a single ruler, but he couldn't call himself king because Romans still hated the word. He presented himself as a senior officer in the service of the state. This show of humility encouraged the Senate to grant him greater authority than they had planned. Then

The death of Julius Caesar, as depicted by 19th-century artist Jean-Léon Gérôme. The Walters Art Museum, Baltimore

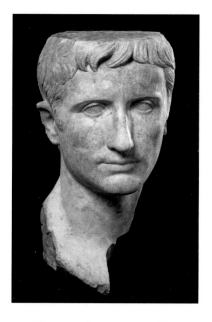

Marble bust of Augustus. The flat part on his head was probably holding a section of his toga, which would have been pulled up to indicate his role as *Pontifex Maximus* (chief priest). All emperors after him held the same title. The Walters Art Museum, Baltimore

he adopted the name Augustus, meaning "favored by the gods," and named himself **emperor**.

The word *emperor*, still used today to refer to Augustus and his successors, simply meant "commander." Historians refer to the first 400 years of the Roman Empire (until Emperor Diocletian) as the **Principate**. During the Principate, many republican institutions continued, even though the emperors gained more and more power.

Rome experienced relative peace under Augustus, a time known as *Pax Romana* (Roman Peace). It meant that the emperor was able to keep peace within the empire, even though he still had to use an army to crush rebels and invaders.

Augustus was also able to expand the empire and restore Roman moral values, including rules to protect marriage and the family. Overall, the Roman people loved him. Some senators mourned the end of the republic, but even they were tired of the long and violent civil wars.

This time of peace and stability was interrupted by two short civil wars, each occurring when an emperor died without leaving a successor. Some emperors, such as Augustus's grandson Caligula and

Caligula's grandson Nero, were cruel and tyrannical. Some of the most respected emperors were Vespasian (AD 69–79), who brought stability to the empire, and Marcus Aurelius (161–180), who is considered the last emperor of the *Pax Romana*.

His son Commodus (161–192), less concerned with defending the empire's borders, began a period of a steady decline, plagued by frequent foreign raids and military rebellions. From 235 to 284, 25 out of 26 emperors were murdered.

Reorganization

In 286, Emperor Diocletian realized the empire was too big to be ruled by one man. He divided it in half, keeping the supervision of the eastern part and assigning the western portion to general Maximian.

The responsibility was large even for two men, so Diocletian chose another commander, Galerius, to assist him. Maximian chose Constantius to do the same for him. The emperors kept the title augustus, while their assistants were known as caesars. According to Diocletian's plans, after 20 years both he and Galerius would retire and leave the crown to their assistants. It was an intelligent and revolutionary plan.

But even Diocletian loved power. He called himself "son

This gigantic head of Constantine the Great is one of the few remaining portions of an enormous statue. Sebastian Lee, iStock

5

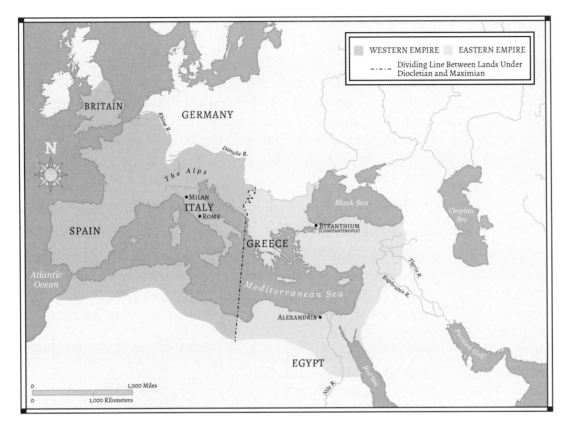

Map of the divided Roman Empire.

According to accounts, before the battle he saw the Greek letters *chi* (X) and *rho* (P) in a dream, which are the first two letters in the name Christ, the Greek equivalent of the Hebrew "Messiah." He painted these letters on his soldiers' shields and attributed his victory to Jesus of Nazareth, known as the Christ, whom he now worshiped as god.

Constantine ruled over the Western Empire, while his ally Licinius ruled the East. In 313, the two emperors agreed that the Christian religion should no longer be outlawed.

The End of the Western Empire

In 376, Rome faced a new problem. Tens of thousands of Goths (a Germanic population) begged the Romans to let them enter the empire to escape a fierce attack from the Asian Huns. The Roman emperor Valens agreed, as long as the Goths converted to Christianity and performed military service. He even gave them free food until they could get settled.

This plan didn't go smoothly. Some Roman officials disliked the Goths and refused to give them food. They also tried to force them into slavery. The Goths rebelled. Violence erupted and the emperor launched a military attack. Confident they would win, in 378 the Romans attacked the Goths at the Battle of Adrianople (in today's Turkey), without waiting for orders. Noticing their disorganization, the Goths responded with full force, killing 40,000 Romans, including the emperor.

of Jupiter" and required his subjects to bow to the ground before him. His claim of divine authority clashed with the growing Christian community, who worshiped a single god. Diocletian's short and bloody campaign to punish rebellious Christians became the fiercest in history.

In 305, Diocletian kept his word and retired, returning to Dalmatia to garden. Maximian retired too. The empire passed to their caesars, who in turn chose new caesars to take their places. This system didn't last long, however, because the rulers began fighting for power.

At this time rose an emperor named Constantine ("the Great") who defeated his rivals at the Milvian Bridge in northern Rome.

The Goths stayed inside the Roman Empire's borders. Most of the time, it was peaceful. Many Romans, however, disliked these foreigners, whose looks, habits, and language were different and uncivilized to Roman eyes, and they launched violent attacks against them.

Finally, in AD 410, a Gothic general named Alaric, angered by unfulfilled Roman promises, led his troops against the city of Rome. At first, his troops surrounded Rome in a **siege**. When attempts to come to an agreement failed, he attacked and robbed the city, destroying buildings.

The Romans were in shock. How could it be? Rome was called the "Eternal City" and had not been attacked by a foreign enemy since 390 BC.

It looked like the end of the world, but it wasn't. For Rome, it was just gradual decay. More Germanic tribes entered Roman territories, and the Roman government withdrew its troops from Britain, Spain, and North Africa. The empire was just too large to manage.

Rome was attacked again in 455 by a Germanic tribe called Vandals. The final attack came in 476, when a Germanic warrior named Odoacer, who had joined the Roman army, captured Rome and removed its last emperor, Romulus Augustus, from power. He then declared himself king of Italy.

Why did the powerful Western Roman Empire come to an end? It's a difficult question to answer, because many of the reasons historians have suggested were also present in the Eastern Roman Empire, which thrived for another 1,000 years, until it was conquered by the Ottomans (Turks) in 1453. One possible answer is that the Western Empire gradually lost the ability to deal with the challenges that came with its size. The Eastern Empire was more manageable and stable.

Nevertheless, Roman culture, laws, habits, and literature continued for centuries, both in the East and the West. Even the conquering tribes appreciated the greatness of Rome and tried to imitate and preserve it.

ROMAN ARCHITECTURE

Roman architects and engineers were resourceful and inventive. Many of their buildings and constructions still stand and have served as models for generations. Some buildings you know were inspired by the architecture of ancient Rome. The White House with its columns looks typically Roman, and the Jefferson Memorial resembles the Roman Pantheon, a temple devoted to all gods.

Roman architecture flourished under Augustus, who boasted he found Rome a city of bricks and left it a city of marble. In reality, the extensive use of bricks and concrete was a Roman innovation that revolutionized Western architecture.

Marble was expensive. It had to be dug out of the sides of mountains through special pits called **quarries**. In Italy, marble was found

Jefferson Memorial. Jim Bowen, Flickr

Pantheon. Roberta Dragan, Wikimedia

mostly in an area about 250 miles northeast of Rome. Even less expensive stone was not widely available.

The Romans discovered that by mixing sand, seawater, and volcanic ash with a white substance called **lime**, they could create a resistant type of concrete. This concrete was so long-lasting, many Roman buildings still stand today, 2,000 years after they were erected. Modern scientists say the secret was in the type of volcanic ash they used and its reaction with seawater.

Houses, Apartments, and Villas

Rome was first a village of huts, similar to those built by other populations in that era. They were made of wood and woven branches plastered with clay, or of mudbricks—blocks of mud mixed with dry grass, leaves, or twigs that were dried in the sun. The roofs were bundles of reeds or straw reinforced with clay. In time, Roman homes became larger and sturdier, built of baked bricks or stone with roof tiles. The Latin word for house or home is *domus*. A *domus* could have one or two floors.

If you went through the front door of one of these larger homes, you would end up in a **courtyard** called an atrium. The roof had an opening in the center with a basin below to collect rainwater. Farther in, there was a courtyard, lined with columns, filled with plants and statues.

Opposite the entrance, another door took you into the living quarters—the dining room, the owners' bedrooms, servants' bedrooms, the kitchen, and storage rooms. Walls were usually brightly colored and decorated, even though the rooms were dim, lit by oil lamps and warmed by **braziers**, which held burning coals.

Windows were rare, small, and didn't let in much light. Glass—first used in the first century AD—was thick and cloudy. Only the wealthy could afford small amounts of glass. Many Romans covered window openings with animal skins kept moist with oil. These let some light in, kept the heat inside during winter, and kept out insects and dust.

The richest citizens had even larger homes, called villas. Sometimes they had more than one: a villa in the city and other villas in the country, sometimes with farms. These homes were often luxurious, with large **frescos** painted directly on the walls and **mosaics** on the floors made from small square stones or colored tiles.

Large scenes were painted on some inside walls, making it appear as if the viewer was looking outside. In some homes, artists painted fake windows, curtains, doors, columns, and even shelves with baskets or bowls of fruit. Romans had few pieces of actual furniture and liked to hide them under cushions and drapes.

One of the most luxurious villas in Italy belonged to the Roman general Lucullus, who lived in the first century BC. His property included hot water springs, private libraries, collections of paintings and statues, large cages filled with birds, pens of wild animals, spacious fish ponds, and impressive gardens for pleasure and for growing fruits and vegetables.

After a while, Rome was too crowded for single homes. Architects began constructing apartment buildings, which they called *insulae*. Initially *insulae* had as many as 12 floors, but the government limited them to 4 or 5. These structures were ingenious and unusual, and visitors to Rome must have wondered how people could live bunched up in those tall buildings.

The poorest people usually lived on the top floors, which were harder to reach and more dangerous during fires and earthquakes. Merchants and artisans lived closer to street level. Overall, these *insulae* were quite uncomfortable. They didn't have running water and the neighbors could be noisy. They were also unsafe and were easily damaged or destroyed. Also, Romans threw their garbage out the windows, so it was unwise to walk near an apartment building. Cities were dirty and messy places to live.

All Roads Lead to Rome

As Rome conquered more territories, roads became increasingly important. They had to be sturdy and efficient, allowing large armies to march to war and messengers to travel speedily from one end of the empire to the other. Romans made their roads as straight as possible. If they found obstacles, they found a way across them. Their roads were so outstanding that many are still in use today.

According to the architect Vitruvius, to build a road the Romans first dug a trench, which they then filled with three layers of building materials: a layer of fist-sized stones, a layer of concrete, and a layer of broken pottery mixed with cement. On top, they laid flat paving stones. To build a road across swampy land, they fortified the sides of the ditch with wood before laying the different materials.

Roman roads were never completely flat. They were slightly curved on top to allow rainwater to flow to the sides, into the fields or small ditches that were dug for that reason.

The old saying "All roads lead to Rome" was actually true during the Roman Empire. In fact, all roads led to a particular spot in the Roman Forum—the *miliarium aureum*, "the golden milestone."

The Via Appia joined Rome to Brindisi, a port on the southeast coast, which was a gateway to the East. This road was so important and well-constructed, it earned the name *Regina viarum* (Queen of roads). John Winder, Flickr

Theaters and Stadiums

The Romans learned from the Etruscans how to build arches, which could be used for bridges and **aqueducts**. Over time they perfected those techniques, becoming master builders. Arches, bridges, and aqueducts were common sights throughout the empire. Roman aqueducts were so well built they are still models for today's structures.

Arches allowed the Romans to build larger and lighter buildings with fewer bricks and stone. One of the most striking uses of arches is in the Roman Colosseum, which was like an open theater. The Colosseum's frame had three rows of arches, one on top of another, topped by a wall with 40 square windows. The columns between the arches and between the windows were meant for decoration.

Stacking one row of arches on another allowed the Romans to build a high structure without making it too heavy, making room for bleachers where people could sit and watch the shows and games. The Greeks built their theaters next to hills and their bleachers directly on the slopes. But these hills were often far from town. The Colosseum was right in the middle of Rome.

The Colosseum took eight years to build. It was completed in AD 80. To mark the occasion, Emperor Titus organized 100 days of

games, including wild animal hunts and wrestling matches between trained fighters known as **gladiators**.

The Colosseum was 150 feet tall (as tall as a 15-story building) and could hold 50,000 people. The architects created 80 entrances to allow everyone to enter or exit peacefully in about 15 minutes. The construction required around 100,000 tons of stone and 300 tons of iron, which was used to clamp the blocks together and keep them in place.

Atop the Colosseum, 240 wooden beams were arranged in the shape of a crown. They held up a huge, thin cover that a team of 100 trained sailors (who had experience with sails) could pull over the structure to protect spectators from the sun or rain.

Beneath the Colosseum there were two floors where the beasts and warriors waited. When their turns came, they were quickly lifted up through a trapdoor with ropes and would appear suddenly in the arena, as if in a magic show.

The Colosseum. Trialsanderrors, Wikimedia Commons

Build a Miniature Roman Road

This indoor activity will give you an idea of how Romans built their roads. If you have a yard and plenty of natural stones and gravel, you can build a small road outside.

ADULT SUPERVISION REQUIRED

Materials

1 pound aquarium river stones (or similar, from nature, as flat as possible)

Medium rectangular plastic container (6 inches by 4¼ inches by 2¾ inches)

Measuring cup

½ cup gravel

3 small bowls or containers

3 egg shells

1½ cup of plaster of paris (read the warnings on the container)

½ cup water

Modeling tool or disposable spoon

Adult helper

1. Divide 1 pound of aquarium river stones into two piles. The second pile should have mostly flat stones, with two or three fewer stones than the other.

2. Lay the first pile of stones on the bottom of a plastic container, spread evenly.

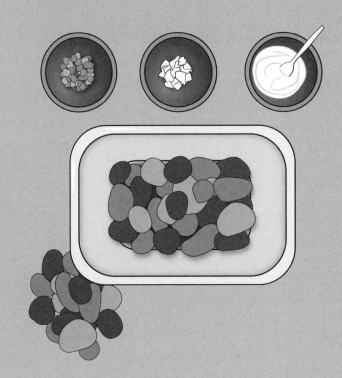

3. Place a ½ cup of gravel in a bowl.

4. Using your hands, crush three egg shells into another bowl. (The broken egg shells substitute for broken pottery.)

5. Mix the plaster of paris with water in the third bowl using a modeling tool or spoon. It should look like pancake batter.

6. Pour half of the plaster over the gravel and stir.

7. Pour the other half of the plaster over the crushed egg shells and stir.

8. Working quickly, use the modeling tool or spoon to spread the gravel mixture over top of the layer of stones in your container.

9. Spread the egg shell mixture on top of the gravel.

10. While the plaster is still soft, lay the flat stones on top, as close as possible to each other. Press the stones down so that they are as flat and even as possible.

11. Let it dry.

12. Wash your hands thoroughly with soap and water to remove any plaster you may have accidentally touched.

13. Once dry, remove this "road" from the container and observe it from the side.

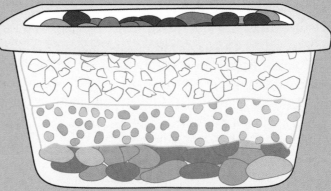

TEMPLES

Early Roman temples followed the Etruscan model: they were built on a raised podium and had a front entrance between columns and closed sides. Others were similar to Greek temples, with columns all around. Unlike the Greeks, Romans built their temples in the main areas of town.

The most original and impressive temple in Rome was the Pantheon, a temple devoted to the worship of all gods. It was begun by Augustus's good friend and adopted son, Agrippa, around AD 25. Throughout the centuries, it has been damaged and remodeled, so the current version is slightly different from the original. Romans believed the Pantheon was built on the exact location where an eagle grabbed Romulus and took him to the gods.

In front of the Pantheon there are 16 50-foot-tall columns: 8 in pink granite and 8 in gray granite, all from Egypt. The actual temple is round, topped by a dome that is an architectural masterpiece. With a 142-foot diameter, it's still the world's largest dome built without reinforced concrete.

If the Romans had constructed the dome with bricks, it would have fallen apart. Instead, they used pure concrete mixed with clay, brick fragments, and a light volcanic stone called **tufa**, with the heaviest materials at the bottom and the lightest at the top. They stopped short of the peak, leaving a hole in the middle (called an oculus, Latin for eye) that lets light into the building.

To prevent rain that falls through the oculus from flooding the building, its floor is carefully sloped to the outside. Later architects added drains to the floor.

In AD 608, the Byzantine emperor Phocas allowed **Pope** Boniface IV to turn the Pantheon into a Christian church. The pope removed the statues of emperors and gods and replaced them with statues of Christian saints. He added an **altar** on one side for celebrating mass but made minimal changes to the building. Today, there are still many original elements to admire.

ROMAN CLOTHING

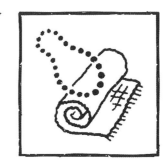

When you watch movies about ancient Rome, Romans often wear long **togas**, with one arm constantly bent to hold up the fabric. But the toga was only one piece of the Roman wardrobe.

Under all their clothes, Romans wore underwear called *subligar,* which means "wrapped underneath." It was a woolen cloth wrapped around the hips like a diaper, to protect the body's intimate parts.

A portion of a third-century mosaic showing three young women engaged in exercise or athletic competitions. NYStevegeer, iStock

Some women also wore a cloth (called *strophium*) around the torso to support their breasts. Some athletes wore only these two articles of clothing.

A **tunic** was worn over the underwear, like a large T-shirt that went down to the knees (for men) and to the feet (for women). It was made of linen or wool—usually beige or cream, the fabric's natural color. Sheep's wool was locally produced, but linen came from Egypt and was expensive. Women's tunics were more colorful and elegant than men's. They were called *stolae,* and were usually held up by two belts, one at the waist and one just below the breasts.

Romans wore their tunics even in bed. They usually had a bath every afternoon (at one of the public bath facilities around town), so they could still be clean by bedtime.

People born in the lower classes—servants and farmers—wore only a tunic and a pair of sandals. Only the rich wore togas, not only because the fabric was expensive but also because wrapping it around the body required someone's help—usually a servant's. After all the wrapping, only one arm of the wearer was free to move around. The other had to be kept slightly raised, to hold up a fold of the fabric.

Togas were a symbol of status. Only Roman males could wear them. They also had distinctive styles to show the rank of the person wearing them. Public magistrates, priests, and boys who had not yet come of age wore a white toga with a purple border (*toga pretexta*). Adult men wore a simple toga of undyed wool. Those in mourning wore gray or brown.

Candidates for elections whitened their togas with chalk as a symbol of purity. This type of toga was called *toga candida* (white toga). The English word *candidate* comes from this custom. The most expensive togas were dyed purple—the color of power—and were worn by emperors and victorious generals on special occasions. Purple dye was costly because it was extracted from a small sea snail called a murex. Collecting the snail and extracting and processing the dye required much time and labor.

At dinner, most Romans set their togas aside and wore either their tunics (at home) or special tunics with a short wrap, called *synthesis*. They were more comfortable than togas, and allowed the men to move freely.

The women's version of the toga was a long, rectangular shawl called a *palla* that wrapped around the body, often covering the head. The *palla* was more colorful than the toga. Sometimes it was embroidered. Rich women could afford expensive fabrics like linen, cotton, and silk, which came from China. If a woman wanted variety, she could take a *palla* to a dyer, who changed its color, making it look brand new.

Clothes and linens were folded and kept in special wooden chests. The Romans had wardrobes, which they invented, but used them to hold precious objects.

On their feet, Romans wore sandals or shoes similar to the ones people wear today, sometimes with little holes punched in them to let air inside. Socks were worn in cold weather. When guests entered a home, a servant took their shoes, washed their feet, and gave them pairs of indoor sandals.

Cleanliness and Beauty

Few Romans had bathtubs inside their homes. Instead, they went daily to the public baths, which were open to rich and poor, men and women. The baths were affordable, and many services were free. In the second century AD, there were 11 large bathing facilities and about 1,000 smaller ones in Rome alone.

People would stay at the baths for hours. Besides pools of hot, cold, and tepid water, many had barber shops, massage parlors, gymnasiums, libraries, restaurants, and lecture halls.

To clean their bodies, the Romans didn't use soap. Instead, they rubbed olive oil on their skin, sometimes mixed with fine white sand, and scraped it off with a curved metal tool called **strigil**. They often did this after bathing or exercising.

Athletes had bundles of strigils attached to rings so they could clean their entire bodies quickly before games, by using one strigil after another. They often had to work together, with one athlete cleaning another. Rich people had their slaves to perform this task.

Like men from nations around them, early Roman men wore beards. The fashion changed around 300 BC, when shaving became

This Roman mosaic, found in the baths at the Sea of Sabratha, bears the inscription *Salvom lavisse* (Washing yourself is good for you). The image shows what was necessary for a good bath: a pair of sandals, strigils, and a bottle of oil.
© Gilles Mermet / Art Resource, NY

Clean Your Skin Like a Roman

Try the strigil method on your skin. Do this activity over a sink or bathtub where oil can be spilled.

Materials

1 teaspoon olive oil

2 teaspoons

1. Make sure you don't have any cuts or sores on your skin. Then pour 1 teaspoon of oil directly from the teaspoon onto your arm or leg.
2. Spread the oil on your skin with your hand.
3. Using the other teaspoon, scrape off the oil. Press just enough to collect the oil onto the spoon.
4. Compare the oil you just collected with oil left on the first teaspoon. Is it still as clear?
5. Collect any remaining oil from your skin.

You can wash the remaining oil off or leave it on your skin. Olive oil is good for your skin.

an expected ritual. **Philosophers** (people who studied and discussed the meaning of life) were one exception. A young man's first shave was considered a rite of passage, and his shaved-off beard was often offered to the gods.

Shaving could be painful; razor blades were not as thin as they are today, and Romans didn't use any ointment or soap. Men must have been glad when, around AD 120, Emperor Hadrian started to wear a beard (allegedly to hide a scar). This meant others could do the same without being accused of being wild **barbarians**.

Normally, men didn't shave themselves. They went to a barber or had a slave do it. Barbers also cut nails, plucked eyebrows, and shaved or waxed other parts of the body. There was a rumor that Emperor Augustus used hot walnut shells to soften the hair on his legs.

Women paid much attention to their hair. Hairstyles were often complicated, involving the use of thin headbands, hairpins, hairpieces, and even needles and thread to keep it all together. During the Imperial era, women's hairstyles imitated those of the emperor's family, so much that scholars today can date statues based on the hairstyle displayed.

Elaborate hairstyles were a sign of wealth because they required the help of another person, showing that the woman could afford a servant and had plenty of time to sit around. Wealthy women could always wear wigs, which were quite popular and made of real hair

Head of a Roman lady from the late first century AD. Fletcher Fund, 1927, Metropolitan Museum of Art, NY

in many colors. Wigs of blonde hair from northern women were especially prized.

Makeup was also especially used by wealthy women, who colored their eyelids, cheeks, and lips with natural ingredients. But natural didn't mean healthy. To get rosy cheeks, Roman women used a paste made of ground cinnabar, a red rock that is a form of mercury sulfite—a toxic mineral that could cause shaking, a shortened life, or sudden death.

ROMAN WRITING

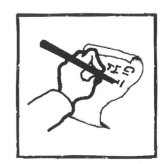

Latin was the official language of the Roman Empire. Though the Romans never made it mandatory for conquered nations to learn Latin, it was essential to know for business or politics within the empire. In Italy, languages like Etruscan gradually disappeared. Highly educated Romans also spoke Greek.

Roman literature flourished in the period from the first century BC to the first century AD. Virgil, one of the greatest poets of all time, lived during this period. His epic poem, the *Aeneid*, tells the legend of Aeneas, the man who escaped the burning city of Troy to land in Italy, where his son, Ascanius, ruled over the future Romans and was the ancestor of Romulus.

Other forms of literature in ancient Rome were theatrical scripts, history books, and **satires**, which highlighted the problems of Rome, its society, and its leaders in clever and humorous ways. Julius Caesar's books about his conquests were bestsellers in his day.

Romans also wrote books on art and science. For example, in the first century AD, architect Vitruvius wrote a 10-volume work on engineering and architecture, and naturalist Pliny the Elder wrote a huge essay on science, with a bonus section on the history of classical art. There were also many political books, and others on how to live well. The famous author and politician Cicero wrote an essay on how to grow old gracefully, one on how to win an election, and another on how to be a good friend.

Of course, books were different from the one you are reading now. They were written on strips of papyrus, which were rolled up around two wooden rods. To read them, one had to unroll the papyrus from one rod and roll it onto the other. As you can imagine, it was difficult to find a particular section of the book. That's why long books such as Vitruvius's were divided into several scrolls.

Roman writing tools. Richard Nicholson of Chester, antiquemaps.com

Write a Letter Like an Ancient Roman

Romans wrote letters a little differently than most people do today, but there might be a familiar touch to them as well!

Materials

Paper

Pen or pencil

1. Read this English translation of a letter by Marcus Tullius Cicero to his wife, Terentia:

   Tullius to his wife Terentia, greetings.

   If you are well, that's good. I am well. Please take very good care of your health. I received a letter telling me you have contracted a fever. Thank you for keeping me up to date about Caesar's letters. Keep doing that. If you need anything, if you have any news, be sure to let me know. Again, take care of yourself. Goodbye.

   Sent on 2 June.

2. Now write a letter. Start with your name, followed by "to," and the name of the person to whom you are writing. Make your names sound Roman. For example, Marcus instead of Mark or Lucas instead of Luke. Girls' names usually ended with an -a, so Megan can be Megana and Emily can be Emilia.

3. Add some form of greeting. Romans often shortened their greetings, using just an "s" or "sal." for *salutem* (greetings) or "s.d." for *salutem dicit* ([the author of this letter] sends his/her greetings) or "s. p. d." for *salutem plurimam dicit* ([the author of this letter] sends many greetings). This is much like the abbreviations people use today in text messages, such as LOL.

4. Wish your friend good health. The formula used by Cicero ("If you are well, that's good. I am well") was sometimes abbreviated in an acronym: S.V.B.E.E.Q.V. (*Si vales, bene est, egoque valeo*). You may create your own acronym, for example: I.H.Y.A.W. ("I hope you are well").

5. Write the rest of the letter.

6. Add a goodbye, called a valediction, at the end. Cicero used *Vale,* which means "Be well."

7. Date your letter. Romans wrote the date when it was given to the messenger. The English word *date* comes from the Latin *data,* which means "given." Usually, Romans wrote just the day and month.

Writers were not well paid and were usually hoping that a **patron** could support them. Some minor poets would set up a booth on a street and offer their services to people who wanted to send a poem to their loved ones, or a letter to anyone. Sometimes they recited their poems out loud, asking for money from passersby, who were not always pleased.

Virgil's patron was Emperor Augustus, who wanted the *Aeneid* to be published as a testimony to Rome's glorious history. Virgil died before finishing, but Augustus insisted the book be published, even though Virgil had left instructions in his will to destroy it. The *Aeneid* became popular and has influenced many poets throughout the centuries.

A patron made sure that an author had good **scribes** to write down his works. Scribes spent all day writing. Once a book was transcribed, it was sent to booksellers.

Stores selling the same type of goods were usually all lined up on one street. Bookstores were no exception. If people wanted a book, they walked down a specific street in Rome, looking at the booksellers' doors for available titles. Sometimes a bookseller would post a portion of a book on his door, like today's websites do.

Books were expensive to purchase, but there were public libraries. During the reign of Trajan, there were 28 libraries in Rome alone. Unlike Egypt, where only scribes and high-ranking officers could read and write, Rome was full of literate people—young and old, men and women.

COMMON LATIN PHRASES

Many Latin phrases are still used today. See how many of these you recognize.

Ad infinitum = To infinity. This is used when something goes on and on, apparently forever.

Carpe diem = Seize the day (or, Grab each opportunity). This is from a poem by Horace.

E pluribus unum = Out of many, one. This phrase is found on the seal of the United States.

Ergo = Therefore.

Et cetera = And others.

Ipso facto = By the fact itself. For example, if you can't resist sweets, you have *ipso facto* a sweet tooth.

Mea culpa = It's my fault.

Quid pro quo = Something for something—a favor for a favor.

Veni, vidi, vici = I came, I saw, I conquered. These words were printed on a wooden poster by Julius Caesar and carried to the streets of Rome after his victory over Pharnaces II of Pontus.

Vice versa = On the other hand.

ROMAN ART AND MUSIC

Initially, Romans imitated Greek art, which many considered the best in the world. Later, they borrowed from other nations, choosing styles of art that best glorified Rome.

Sculpture

Sculpture played an important part in Roman life. Anyone who could afford a nice house or villa wanted to decorate it with sculptures—of themselves or their ancestors. Temples were full of statues of gods and goddesses, created from wood or marble and covered with precious materials, such as gold and ivory.

A main goal of Roman art was to remind others of Rome's great victories and its heroes. Romans were not as concerned as Greeks with ideal beauty. During the republican age, they didn't mind showing wrinkles, long noses, and sunken cheeks. In fact, some men liked to look rough and rugged. It showed they were hardworking and honest. If they wanted their statues to look glorious, they added rich clothes and serious expressions.

The **bust**, a sculpture of a person's head and shoulders, was quite popular in Rome. Sometimes when people died, their loved ones made wax impressions of their faces and kept these masks or used them as molds to create true-to-life busts.

Some leaders, like Julius Caesar and Augustus, preferred to show themselves without flaws. Caesar was bothered by growing bald and asked sculptors to add more hair than he really had. Later emperors returned to the realistic style, allowing us to see them for what they were: mostly strong but unrefined soldiers.

Another common type of sculpture in ancient Rome was the **relief**, where a design is raised above the background. Relief sculptures were found everywhere in the Roman Empire, especially on monuments built to commemorate victories, such as triumphal arches. The relief on the Trajan Column, a 98-foot-tall monument, includes 2,662 figures in 155 different scenes. It was built by Emperor Trajan to celebrate his conquest of Dacia, in Eastern Europe.

A portion of the Trajan Column. The column was built with 21 blocks of marble and was originally brightly colored. Gary Campbell-Hall, Flickr

Tell Your Life Story on a Roman Column

The Trajan Column is like a huge winding scroll that goes up to the sky, telling the story of the conquest of Dacia like a giant comic strip. Use the same idea to tell a story of your life.

Materials

Pencil

Empty paper towel roll

Thin markers

1. Think of 10 or 11 scenes from your life. For example, your birth, your first day of school, the birth of a brother or sister, a move to another home, your first soccer practice, or your first day with a best friend.

2. Use the pencil to draw a line over the diagonal marks on the roll.

3. Holding the paper roll with one hand, draw in pencil the different scenes, one after the other, starting on the lowest corner of the strip. You can use stick figures. Each scene should be about 2 inches wide. (Divide the scenes by drawing a line between them.

4. Use thin markers to color the scenes.

5. Give your name to the column (for example, Tyler Column or Megan Column).

Paintings and Mosaics

Most Roman paintings have been destroyed. A few were preserved in Pompeii and Herculaneum, two cities that were buried in AD 79 by thick layers of ash and mud from the volcano Vesuvius. These paintings are remarkable for their realism, color, and ability to portray movement, depth, and distance. Some covered whole walls, as if to make viewers believe they could see through them to the scenes outdoors.

Mosaics were better preserved than paintings, because they were created by attaching small squares of tile, marble, stone, or glass to a surface (usually walls or floors) so firmly they could hardly be removed. These little squares were called *tesserae*, from the Greek word for "four." In some cases, the artists added some tiny seashells.

Many wall paintings and mosaics portrayed the natural world, especially gardens and animals. Stories from Roman history or **mythology** were also common subjects.

Black-and-white mosaics became popular in the second century AD on signs and in bathrooms. Merchants placed mosaics in front of their shops to advertise their goods. Other mosaics were meant as warnings: *Inbide, calco te* (Envious one, I trample on you) or *Cave canem* (Beware of the dog).

First-century Roman wall painting of a glass bowl with fruit. Erich Lessing / Art Resource, NY

Ancient Roman mosaic in Pompeii, Italy, with the writing: CAVE CANEM. Mitch Barrie, Flickr

ROMAN MUSIC

There are no samples of music played by ancient Romans, but they certainly used instruments throughout their long history, from simple flutes, bagpipes, and trumpets, to complex organs. Most of their instruments were adopted from neighboring nations or from people they conquered.

Music was played in temples, in theaters, during festivals or military parades, and at private parties. Trumpets came in different shapes and forms and were used in war and at funerals. War trumpets were usually G-shaped.

Musicians played an important role in Roman society because music was a regular part of public and private life. Bands of traveling musicians toured the streets of Rome and other cities, together with jugglers and acrobats. They usually played simple instruments, such as flutes, cymbals, and tambourines. There were even a few one-man shows, where one street musician played many instruments at once.

First-century BC Roman mosaic showing street musicians playing the flute, the tambourine, and a type of castanets.
© Vanni Archive/ Art Resource, NY

Warn Your Friends with a Roman Mosaic

Create a mosaic warning sign using paper instead of tiles.

Materials

Pencil

Piece of cardboard (any size)

Bag of mosaic paper squares cut from old magazines or construction paper

Scissors

Glue stick

1. With a pencil, draw a picture of your pet on a piece of cardboard.

2. Add a Latin warning.

   - If you are drawing your dog, you can write, *Cave canem*.
   - It you are drawing a cat, *Cave felem*.
   - If a fish, *Cave piscem*.
   - If a bird, *Cave avem*.
   - If a turtle, *Cave testudinem*.
   - If a hamster, *Cave cricetum*.
   - If a rabbit, *Cave cuniculum*.
   - If you don't have a pet, draw yourself or one of your siblings, and write *Cave* plus the name.

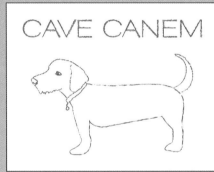

3. Choose what colors you want to use (black, gray, or brown for a dog or cat; orange for a goldfish, etc., and another color for the background). Sort the paper squares so you have a pile for each color you need.

4. With the glue stick, apply glue to a portion of the picture.

5. Lay the appropriate tiles on that portion, one by one, keeping them as close as possible to each other without overlapping. Cut the tiles in half or quarters to fill small spaces.

6. Repeat for other portions of your picture, including the words and background, until your mosaic is complete.

ROMAN RELIGION

Ancient Romans worshiped many gods, often similar to those worshiped by the ancient Greeks. The 12 main gods were called *dii consentes*: Jupiter (king of the gods and protector of the state), Mars (god of war), Neptune (god of the sea), Apollo (god of the arts), Mercury (messenger of the gods), Vulcanus (god of fire), Minerva (goddess of wisdom and military strategies), Venus (goddess of beauty and love), Diana (goddess of hunting), Ceres (goddess of fertility), Juno (wife of Jupiter and protector of women and children), and Vesta (goddess of the home).

Besides these and other public gods, each Roman family had a group of minor personal gods, called Lares and Penates, who watched over the home. The Lares protected the home and family, and the Penates watched over the family's welfare, unity, and prosperity. Each homeowner built a small shrine to these gods, and paid respect to them every morning. The Penates' shrines were kept near the fireplace in the center of the home.

As Rome grew and conquered new lands, it often adopted foreign gods. Egyptian gods and goddesses were especially popular, because they had been around for thousands of years. Some of these religions included stricter rules than Roman worship, which varied from place to place.

Generally, Romans were tolerant of other religions. Initially, however, they didn't understand Christians, whose religion sounded new, strange, and dangerous. Many Romans believed Christians angered the traditional Roman gods and brought destruction to the state. This mostly changed when Emperor Constantine made Christianity legal, and later gave Christians special privileges.

THE AFTERLIFE

Like the Egyptians before them, Romans believed there was a happy place after this life—the Elysian Fields—but it was reserved for the few who had done something exceptional. The souls of common people went to Hades, a gloomy and dark world.

The spirits of the dead (called *manes*) were also allowed to wander graveyards, which were built outside the city gates. Many tomb **inscriptions** included short summaries of the person's life, or messages the dead would have wanted to tell the living. Here are some examples:

"Hey, you who are passing by, come here, rest a while. Are you shaking your head? Yet, you will have to come here too."

"I lived as I wanted. I don't know why I am dead."

"Here is buried Leburna, drama teacher, who lived about one hundred years. I have died many times, but never like this. To you up there I wish well."

ROMAN GOVERNMENT AND WARFARE

In the Roman republic, laws and military decisions were discussed and approved in the Senate, a permanent group of about 300 men who were chosen by the censors. The censors had the task of counting the Roman population, what is today called a "census." They knew who was mature enough to make wise decisions, and wealthy enough to care for their property and, as a result, for the country.

The Senate made military decisions and debated and approved laws. It also elected and supervised two consuls who led the army and enforced the laws. Since Rome was a republic, the people were involved in decision making, but they had to be free men and full citizens of legal age. Citizens who were not from rich and powerful families could only vote yes or no on proposals and were not allowed to participate in debates.

In times of great emergency, the Senate could elect a dictator. The word simply meant "someone who gives orders." Dictators swore a solemn oath to give up power after six months. Each dictator had an assistant, called "Master of the Horse."

The Latin acronym SPQR stood for Senatus Populusque Romanus, which means "The Senate and the Roman people." Today, Italians give funny interpretations to the acronym, such as Sono Pazzi Questi Romani (These Romans Are Crazy). J. Miers, Wikimedia Commons

As the Romans expanded their territory, Rome created new governmental positions, such as **governors**, who ruled the distant provinces; **questors**, who took care of financial matters; and **ediles**, who ran the city, including the building and maintenance of streets, bridges, and aqueducts, and the staging of festivals and games. Governors and army commanders had to make many decisions on their own, because it could take months for a letter to travel from some areas of the empire to Rome and back.

At the time of elections, the candidates painted advertisements on city walls, as they do in today's campaigns. Many of these sound normal ("Gaius Julius Polybius for edile. He will get you good bread"). Others may have been written by the candidate's rivals ("The late-night drinkers unanimously support Marcus Cerrinius Vatia for edile"). Painting over a campaign sign to change its message was also common. Someone wrote under his, "If you deliberately deface this sign, may you fall seriously ill."

Design a Coin for a President or Governor

Besides being used for trade, coins sent a message. The Roman Empire was so big that most people never saw the emperor, but they could see his face stamped on one side of their coins. On the other side, coins often had a symbol of the emperor's power: a chariot, a ship, a horse rider, a fierce or mythological animal, or a temple. When Augustus conquered Egypt, he minted a coin with the picture of an alligator (a symbol of Egypt) and the writing, "Egypto Capta" (Conquered Egypt). Design a coin for a president, governor, class president, mayor, school principal, or other leader you respect. Or, choose a hero from a fantasy book or superhero movie.

Materials

½ sheet of letter-size paper

Drawing compass or a round object to trace

Pencil

Scissors

Glue

1. Fold a half-sheet of paper in half crosswise to create two sections.

2. Draw a 3-inch-diameter circle in the middle of the left section using a compass. If you don't have a compass, trace a round object about 3 inches in diameter, such as a coffee mug.

3. Do the same on the right section of the paper.

4. Draw a picture of your chosen leader in the first circle. Write his or her name under the picture inside the circle.

5. In the other circle, draw a picture of something that characterizes this person, or perhaps a symbol of the country, state, city, or school that this person represents. Add the name of the place and its motto, or make up a motto.

6. Cut out the two circles and glue them to each other to create a mock coin.

Roman Warfare

Romans had to learn how to fight from the very beginning. They lived in one of the most fertile places in Italy, in a strategic commercial location, and so they were often the target of hostile neighbors. At first they didn't have the best tactics or training, but eventually Rome created one of the most powerful armies of any time.

Early Roman soldiers bought their own armor and weapons, so landowners often had the best equipment. Those who could afford a horse fought in the **cavalry**. They typically served as long as a war lasted and then went home. Wars later became so frequent and far from Rome that soldiers had to leave their homes for years at a time. This was difficult for property owners.

There were, however, many people who saw benefits to serving in battle. In 107 BC, Consul and General Gaius Marius allowed poor citizens to join the army, where they would receive weapons from the state and earn a piece of land when they were done. Being a soldier became a career. Soldiers trained all the time, not just when there was a call to war.

Different generals added benefits to get the best men for their armies. Soldiers became particularly loyal to one general rather than the empire. This attitude was dangerous to Roman unity and led to civil wars. When Augustus became emperor, he created a single Roman army with a unified standard and a common devotion to Rome and its emperor. The armor, weapons, and customs of Roman soldiers you see in most movies are from the time of Augustus or later.

Roman Armor

Initially, Roman armor was simple: a helmet, a shield, and a **cuirass**, composed of a breastplate and backplate joined together. This cuirass was heavy and expensive, so Romans preferred to use something lighter. When soldiers had to provide their own armor, many hung a metal plate across their chests or went without protection. Some men could afford **mail** armor, made up of chain links, a style copied from the Gauls.

The type of armor you see in most movies is what **legionnaires** wore, starting in the middle of the first century AD, and was made with rectangular metal plates tied together with leather strings. It weighed about 25 or 30 pounds but was flexible like an accordion and covered more of the body than a cuirass.

Helmets also changed. Initially, soldiers wore whatever helmet they could afford. They were usually round and made of bronze or iron, with a longer piece in back to cover the neck and two pieces hanging down over the cheeks. The ears were not covered because soldiers had to hear their commander's orders.

Some helmets had black or purple feathers, a crest of horsehair, or a piece of fur tied around the helmet. These decorations helped an officer quickly recognize his soldiers. The familiar red crest came after the armor was standardized and could be small or large, according to rank.

Early shields were round or oval with decorative metal at the center. This was called the umbo, from the Latin word for belly button. Soldiers held shields with their left hands, using a leather strap on the back. In battle, shields could be used to both defend and attack. A soldier could push it against the enemy, causing him to lose his balance. He could also use a shield to stop the enemy's arm from reaching his sword, or block the enemy's weapon.

Large, rectangular shields came later and were often decorated with eagle's wings and lightning bolts. These shields covered most of the body. A group of soldiers could also march together, holding their shields on all sides and overhead. This formation, known as testudo (or turtle) was especially useful when approaching a wall, because it protected the soldiers from arrows and stones that came from every direction.

Spears were the Romans' main offensive weapons, initially used for thrusting into the enemy, not for throwing. They were made of wood with a sharp metal point on one end. A metal spike was on the other end as a counterweight, and in case the spear tip broke off.

Legionnaires' spears were heavier than those carried by the auxiliaries (foreign recruits who didn't have Roman citizenship). Heavy spears could do a lot of damage. Even if the enemy stopped them with their shields, the spears would became stuck and weigh down the enemy, preventing him from fighting freely.

For close combat, Romans used a short sword, called *gladius*. Soldiers were trained to hit the stomach, where there are no bones. Other populations had longer swords, which they swung over their heads, but in close combat the Romans could pierce their stomachs while they rotated their swords.

Everyone in the army wore the same footwear: leather sandals with a thick, strong sole. During the winter, they wore socks. When they marched from one place to another, they wore a cloak that could be used as a blanket. Besides weapons, they brought axes and shovels to remove obstacles and build camps. Roman soldiers spent most of their time digging and chopping.

They also carried covered metal bowls and small pots for cooking, and flint stones to light fires, all bundled with clothes on a pole held over their shoulders.

Organization and Strategy

The organization of the Roman army changed over time. When Augustus was emperor, the army's main unit was the **legion**, which included 4,800 men. Each legion was divided into 10 cohorts, and every cohort was made up of 6 centuries (*centuria*) of 80 men each. And each **century** was divided into 10 groups of 8 men.

Roman soldiers marched a lot, from one place to another. At night, they set up camp and built fortifications, digging at least one ditch (called *vallum*) around the camp. Each soldier knew exactly what to do and where each tent was to be pitched. If an army stayed in one place for a longer time, they built a stronger fort, which included wooden buildings, such as houses for officers, barracks for soldiers, a hospital, a storage place, and a bathhouse.

Romans often camped in front of enemy forces and waited for them to make the first move. A trumpet announced the start of battle. Roman soldiers were trained to line up quickly in formation—usually three lines of **infantry** with the cavalry at their sides.

The army had several standard-bearers who held up symbols of Roman honor to inspire the soldiers. There were three main types of standards. The eagle was the most valuable, initially made of silver but later gold. It was held with great reverence and was protected at all times.

Testudo formation. Hans Splinter, Flickr

Create a Roman Standard for Your Family or Classroom

*To create a **signum** for your family or classroom, start by counting the victories you have achieved—accomplishments or awards and recognitions. This activity includes three discs to symbolize three victories, but yours can be different. Use a longer stake if needed.*

Materials

2 medium round paper plates

Pencil

Black marker

Scissors

Stapler

6 round dessert paper plates

Garden stake, 4 feet long

White glue

1. Place a medium paper plate on a clean surface and place your left hand flat on it. If you are left-handed, use your right hand instead.

2. Trace around your hand with a pencil.

3. Remove your hand, and retrace the line with a black marker.

4. On a second medium plate, draw a laurel wreath around the border with a marker, 1 inch wide at most.

5. Cut out the wreath.

6. Cut out the hand.

7. Position the hand in the wreath as shown and staple in place.

8. Lay a small paper plate on a clean surface, face up. Top it with another plate, face down, then staple the edges of the plates together until they're secure.

9. Do the same with two more pairs of plates.

10. Lay a garden stake on a flat surface. Attach the hand to the top of the stake with white glue. Press firmly.

11. Attach the other plates beneath the hand, in a row.

12. Hold your standard proudly and be ready to explain what the plates represent.

The *vexillum*, a square piece of cloth with symbols on it, marked the commander's position. Units also held up a golden image of the emperor to remind the soldiers of their loyalty oath.

Each century had a *signum*, a long pole with disks for the century's victories. On top of each *signum* was an ornamental spearhead or an image of a raised hand. The symbolic meaning of these pieces is not clear.

Standard-bearers usually wore animal skins over their uniforms—arms and legs included—with their heads inside the animal's head.

Once the signal was given, the cavalry would charge, throwing a tempest of javelins against the enemy to break up their formation. The infantry followed with short swords. If the enemy fled, often after 20 minutes, the infantry would let them go, but the cavalry would ride ahead to get in their way.

Romans were not expert in naval battles and didn't have a strong fleet until the third century BC, when they copied a Carthaginian ship. In naval war, they had three options: board the enemy ship, ram it, or attack it with fiery darts. The last two methods destroyed the ship and everything on board. Boarding was the best way to conquer a ship and take its goods.

The Senate gave victorious commanders the honor of leading triumphal processions through the streets of Rome, which ended at the Temple of Jupiter. Commanders would ride chariots, wearing the royal symbols of Jupiter, with people cheering along the way.

The processions included displays of the riches taken and chained leaders of the conquered nations. Many emperors raised triumphal arches as lasting reminders of the greatness of their country and its leaders.

Romans believed that war was a sacred duty, blessed by the gods, for the honor and protection of their country. Each declaration of war was pronounced in the Campus Martius of Rome with a series of ceremonial rites performed by Roman priests—including hurling a ceremonial spear into an area that symbolized the enemy's territory.

WHY THE ROMAN ARMY WAS POWERFUL

The Roman army was successful because of the remarkable attitude of its soldiers and commanders. The Latin word *virtus* was used to describe their courage, military skill, and undying loyalty to country and fellow soldiers. The ideal of *virtus* was instilled in the minds of Romans from an early age through stories of heroism.

Above all, Roman soldiers refused to give up. They willingly fought in many different conditions, from the Sahara desert to the cold forests of Britain, and they learned from their mistakes and their enemies' tactics.

The Roman army was ordered and disciplined. A soldier who fell asleep at his post or who stole from another soldier was beaten to death. Men knew this when they enlisted. There were exceptions—Julius Caesar used these drastic measures only in cases of desertion or mutiny—but the training of soldiers was always strenuous, and instant obedience was expected.

Finally, the Romans were supported by their large population. Unlike most ancient cities, Rome grew by allowing allies, conquered enemies, and freed slaves to obtain Roman citizenship. More citizens meant more able-bodied soldiers.

ROMAN DAILY LIFE

The daily life of ancient Romans depended on their status: whether they were rich or poor, enslaved or free, men or women, farmers or city dwellers. Some things, however, were common to all and changed little over the length and span of the empire. Even conquered people eventually adopted Roman customs.

Family Life

A typical Roman family included father, mother, children, grandparents, and slaves. The father was the head of the family and had power of life and death over the other members. Women were under the authority first of their fathers, then of their husbands. Widows were freed but were often poor because they rarely received any inheritance. Typically, they remarried.

Many women were involved in their husbands' work. An artisan's wife helped in the shop, and a politician's wife entertained guests and strengthened useful friendships. Well-educated women were admired.

Children learned basic skills at home until they were seven. In rich families, a slave did this initial instruction, then the boys attended teachers' homes, which worked like small schools. Boys had to learn to speak well in public to advance their political careers.

Girls' educations focused on skills that were needed at home: taking care of the household, raising children, and (for rich girls) directing slaves. Some received a superior education and enjoyed both Latin and Greek literature.

Children wrote on wax tables with a pointed metal tool called a stylus. Wax tablets could be erased by scraping them. Young students often used wooden tables with engraved letters and numbers for tracing practice. To count, they used an abacus—an ancient instrument with sliding beads. Around the age of 13 or 14, many boys traveled to other countries, especially Greece, to further their educations.

Boys were usually trained in their father's occupation. Sons of senators followed their fathers to the forum and listened to meetings from outside. Boys from noble families trained together for war, learning to throw a javelin, use a sword, and ride a horse.

Romans at Work

In the early days of Rome, most of its citizens were farmers and shepherds. As the cities grew, artisans and merchants produced and transported goods for restaurants and travelers. Artisans often lived behind or above their workshops, where they produced and sold their goods.

Besides being politicians, better-educated Romans were lawyers, teachers, architects, and engineers. Without formal degrees, they worked to earn good reputations.

WHAT'S IN A NAME?

Ancient Roman men had three names: the *praenomen*, like the modern first name; the *nomen gentilicum*, for the person's clan or family; and the *cognomen*, a nickname telling something about the person. For example, Cicero meant "chickpea," Scipio "rod," and Agrippa "born feet first." A *cognomen* was either inherited from the parents or given by the community. Sometimes, an extra nickname called an *agnomen* was added when someone did something out-standing. Publius Cornelius Scipio received the extra name Africanus after his victory over Carthage.

The first names Titius, Gaius, and Sempronius were so common that they became a set phrase to mean "just about anyone," like the English "Tom, Dick, and Harry."

Initially, Romans used mostly the first two names, then all three, and later just the *cognomen*. That's why people today speak of Scipio, Caesar, and Cicero, instead of using their full names.

Women had only one name. Since they didn't vote or hold public office, one name was sufficient inside the fam-ily. A woman's name was often an adaptation of her father's family name. For example, the daughters born to Mark Antony and Octavia were both named Antonia. How did they tell them apart? One was Antonia Maior ("the older") and the other Antonia Minor ("the younger").

Initially, there were no doctors in Rome. The parents took care of their families with folk remedies. Later, doctors arrived from Greece. Greek slaves were admired for their medical knowledge. Once freed, they worked as private doctors.

Cicero wrote a letter on Roman occupations. Of all the professions, he thought, "none is better than agriculture, none more profitable, none more delightful, none more becoming to a freeman." Agriculture taught virtues Romans valued, such as diligence and thrift. That's why many generals and politicians retired to farms.

Fun and Games

Entertainment was important to ancient Romans. Children liked to play, and many of their toys looked like yours today: dolls, balls, marbles, miniature carts, spinning tops, and even yo-yos. Girls kept their dolls (often with fake jewels and a small wardrobe) until their wedding days. Boys played with slingshots, bows and arrows, and hobbyhorses. Some games, like hide-and-seek, tag, blind man's bluff, jump rope, tic-tac-toe, knucklebones, and board games were played by everyone. Some homes had swings for young and old.

Men often met outside their homes to watch games and observe court trials, which were held outdoors in the forum. The steps of Basilica Julia (once in the Roman Forum) are still etched with board games such as tic-tac-toe, or squares for games similar to chess or checkers.

Romans loved a variety of ball games. In one popular game, three people stood at three corners of an imaginary triangle and hit a ball toward one another with the palms of their hands. The player who let the ball fall on the ground lost.

They also had theaters for plays, **amphitheaters** where trained gladiators wrestled against each other or wild beasts, and stadiums for chariot races. The biggest amphitheater in Rome was the Colosseum, and the largest stadium the Circus Maximus. Gladiatorial games were

Play a Children's Walnut Game

*Children in ancient Rome used nuts (especially walnuts) as toys. That's why they called
the passage from youth to adulthood as **nuces relinquere** (leaving the nuts).
This game is for two players.*

Materials

Chair

28-by-14-inch piece of cardboard

Small piece of playdough (optional)

Walnuts (at least 14)

1. Place the chair so that there is at least 3 feet of space in front of it.

2. Lean a 28-by-14-inch piece of cardboard against the front of the chair at an incline. If needed, use a little playdough or tape to the bottom to keep it in place.

3. Line up eight walnuts 2 inches from the front of the cardboard.

4. Give each player three nuts.

5. Standing behind the chair, the first player holds a nut at the top of the cardboard, then lets go.

6. The goal is to knock the line of walnuts out of place. Any nuts knocked out of place then belong to the first player, together with the nut he or she rolled. If no nuts were hit, the player must leave his or her nut on the ground.

7. The second player does the same.

8. Continue alternating players until there are no more nuts on the ground.

9. Count how many nuts each player has.

10. Now repeat, but let the second player roll first.

11. When the second game ends, add the scores from both games. The player with the highest total score wins.

violent and bloody, and the Romans loved them. They had favorite gladiators, like today's movie stars, and rooted for them from the stands.

Dice games were popular among friends. Men played them at home, in taverns (eating places), and in military fortresses between battles. They were so common that Emperor Claudius wrote a book on the rules of dice play.

Ancient Romans had many festivals throughout the year. Some were local, and some were observed across the empire. Most celebrations were religious, dedicated to the different gods.

The festival called Ludi (which means "games") started as two days in September and grew until it lasted from September 4 to 19.

During this festival, all public games were free—chariot races, gladiator fights, sports, and mock naval battles.

The most popular holiday was the Saturnalia, celebrated for several days starting December 17 to honor the god Saturn. It marked the approach of the winter solstice (December 25 in the Julian calendar). It was a time of fun, play, lit candles, and gifts. During the holiday, some restrictions were lifted—public gambling was allowed, women fought in the arena, and slaves were treated as equal. It was also a dangerous time, not only because people drank too much but also because some people robbed homes and shops while their owners were busy feasting.

ROMAN FOOD

Initially the food eaten in Rome was grown locally, but as the borders expanded, Romans imported more of what they ate. Most of the grain consumed in Rome came from Egypt.

Breakfast was usually abundant. Traditional breakfasts were bread, cheese, fresh or dried fruit, and honey. It could also include leftovers. For lunch, many men went to a *popina,* a fast-food restaurant common in the Roman world. In Pompeii, remains of about 200 have been found. In a *popina,* men ate bread, meat, fish, eggs, cheese, and beans. There were always olives, fruit, and lots of wine.

Romans discovered an efficient way to make olives edible. Olives straight from the tree are extremely bitter. To debitter them, ancient populations soaked them in saltwater, repeating the process several times, but this could take months. By adding wood ashes to the saltwater, Romans could shorten the process to a few hours. They also added different ingredients while pickling the olives—from oil, vinegar, and herbs to elaborate recipes using wine, grape juice, and cypress leaves.

After lunch, most Romans didn't return to work. Shops opened early and closed around noon, so people went to the public baths and then dinner. If they had guests, dinner was as early as four in the afternoon, because no one wanted to travel back home in the dark. Since lunch was a small meal, by this time people were hungry.

Romans organized banquets more often than people do today. On these occasions, they brought out several courses of food. Most of the food, such as bread, roasted meat, and fruit, could be eaten by hand. Romans liked foods that were spicy or sweet, sometimes both flavors in the same dish.

Wine was common, inexpensive, and often mixed with water to make it last longer. Ice (from snow) was popular. Roman merchants carried it from the mountains and kept it in underground storage rooms covered with straw to keep it from melting. Some Romans complained that it was more expensive than wine.

Most dishes were seasoned with a salty sauce called *garum,* which was made by leaving some small fish (or even just their insides) to ferment for days in the hot sun. After the fish had dissolved, the mush was passed through a sieve, leaving only a liquid. It might sound unappealing, but *garum* is actually coming back among food lovers.

Wealthy Romans enjoyed impressing their guests with unusual or creative dishes. A merchant named Trimalchio served a rabbit with wings added to make it look like a creature from Greek mythology, and small birds stuck with thorns to resemble sea urchins.

Lucullus was the most famous Roman food lover. He had the best chefs and ate like a king, even when he dined alone. Once, when his chef brought him a small dinner because there were no guests,

Serve a Plate of Roman *Frictilia*

Apicius taught his readers to make little strips of fried dough called frictilia. *This recipe has been passed on from family to family over the centuries and is still enjoyed today in the Italian traditional versions called* chiacchiere *(pronounced kiahk-keh-reh) or frappe.*

ADULT SUPERVISION REQUIRED

Materials

1 cup flour

Cutting board

2 eggs

Fork

2 tablespoons olive oil

Rolling pin

Ruler (optional)

Butter knife

Vegetable oil

2 plates

Paper towel

Spatula

Honey

Adult helper

1. Place 1 cup of flour on a clean cutting board, forming a small hill.

2. With your fingers, create a hole in the middle of the hill (forming a volcano).

3. Break 2 eggs into the hole and mix well with a fork, gathering the surrounding flour as you go.

4. Add olive oil and keep mixing. Continue to gather more flour until you get a firm dough.

5. Knead the dough with your hands. Use the palm of your hands for pressure. The dough should take the shape of a firm, smooth ball. If it's sticky, add a little flour.

6. Let it rest for half an hour.

7. Use a rolling pin to flatten the dough as thin as you can on the cutting board. You may want to divide it and flatten one piece at a time.

8. Cut the dough into strips about 1½ inches wide and 4 inches long.

9. With an adult helping, pour vegetable oil in a frying pan or fryer and heat until it boils.

10. Have the adult place the strips of dough in the oil and let them fry until golden.

11. Line a plate with paper towels.

12. When the strips are ready, use the spatula to carefully remove them from the oil and place them on the plate.

13. Once all the strips are cooked and drained of excess oil, move them to another plate and dress them with honey. Enjoy!

Lucullus scolded him, saying, "Don't you know? Today Lucullus dines with Lucullus!" On another occasion, he invited Cicero and Pompey, two famous politicians, and told his servants to set the table in the Apollos Room. They understood immediately, and brought out a fantastic meal of lobster and peacock.

Try an Ancient Roman Spread

A Roman poet—some believe it was Virgil—wrote a short story about a farmer who woke up and looked around for something to eat. He could only find bread and a piece of cheese. Wanting variety, he went to his garden and picked garlic, celery, arugula, and cilantro. He put it all in a mortar and ground it together. Cheese mixed with herbs or spices was a common meal in ancient Rome. Both sheep and goat cheeses were popular. This recipe uses Romano cheese, which is made with sheep milk, and is probably similar to what the farmer had. It also uses a food processor instead of the farmer's mortar and pestle.

Materials

Stalk of celery

4 arugula leaves

2 sprigs of cilantro

Clove of garlic

Small blender or food processor

2 tablespoons grated Romano cheese

1 tablespoon olive oil

Spoon

Bowl

Butter knife

Pita bread (or other flat bread)

1. Wash celery, arugula, and cilantro and place it inside a blender.

2. Peel a clove of garlic and add it to the vegetables.

3. Blend for a few seconds. Try to get the vegetables as pureed as possible.

4. Add grated Romano cheese and blend again.

5. While the ingredients are blending, slowly add a spoonful of olive oil.

6. Check to see if the mixture is smooth. If not, **turn off the blender** and use a spoon to scrape it off the sides of the blender onto the center, and blend again.

7. Repeat step 6 as many times as needed.

8. Once smooth, remove it from the blender with the spoon and place it in a bowl.

9. Tear off a piece of bread. Using the butter knife, spread a little mixture on it.

10. Share with others. Do you like it?

Roman cooks created many versions of this recipe, and you can do the same. You may want to try soft goat cheese or another combination of vegetables. This recipe is similar to Italian pesto.

PART II: THE ETRUSCANS

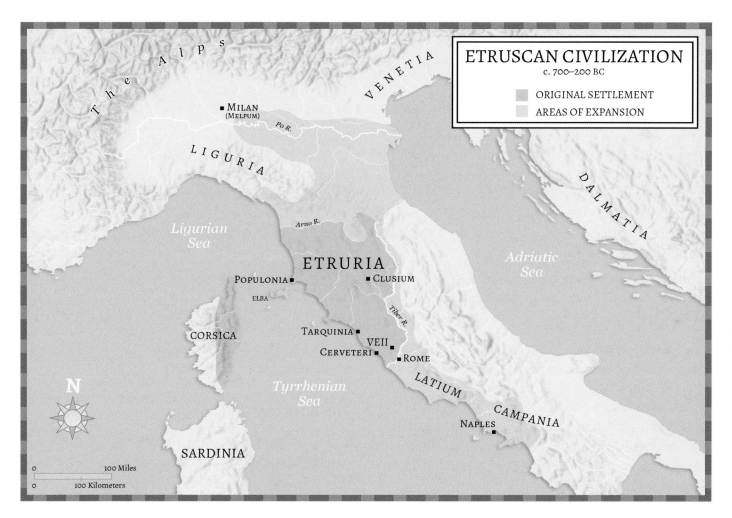

Map of Etruria at the time of its fullest expansion.

ETRUSCAN HISTORY

In 900 BC, Italy was home to a mixture of independent tribes with many different languages and customs. The Etruscans were the strongest and most refined. Some parts of their culture are still mysterious, including their writing, which has never been fully **deciphered**. By studying the Etruscans' tombs and temples and by reading what was written about them, archaeologists and historians have discovered enough to present a fascinating picture of this ancient and intriguing people.

The Etruscans Flourish

Some experts think the Etruscans came from the ancient region of Turkey, while others believe they were native to Italy. There is debate because the Etruscans' culture and language were very different than those of the populations around them.

The Etruscans initially settled in the area between two Italian rivers, the Arno and the Tiber. Later, they expanded north into the Po Valley and south to the region around Naples. Many of today's Italian cities were built by the Etruscans.

The word *Etruscan* comes from the name the Romans gave these people: Tursci (or Turci). The Etruscans called themselves Rasena, which means "people." The Greeks called them Tyrrheni. Because of this, the sea next to their territory became known as Tyrrhenian Sea.

The Etruscans' region, known as Etruria, was filled with valuable natural resources: a rich vegetation, fruitful mines for the extraction of metals and salt, and easy access to the rivers and the sea, where they could fish and sail their trading ships.

Between the sixth and the fourth centuries BC, the Etruscans were famous all over Europe for their wealth, engineering skills, and artwork, including jewelry and pottery. Many of their cities regularly received visitors and merchants from other nations.

Etruscans and Romans had alternating periods of war and peace. The last three of Rome's kings were Etruscan. After the last of these, Tarquinius Superbus, was expelled, there was a long series of battles between these two populations.

The Etruscans Decline

In 396 BC the Romans sacked the Etruscan city of Veii, killed most of its inhabitants, and took over its territory. Around the same year, the Celts, who lived mostly in northern Europe, defeated an Etruscan army at Melpum (today's Milan) and settled in the Po Valley. Suddenly, the Etruscans were seriously threatened from both north and south.

Given a choice, they allied with the Romans, who shared a similar culture and provided greater security. In 390 BC, when the Celts attacked the city of Rome, the Etruscan town of Cerveteri gave shelter to Roman priests and priestesses and their sacred symbols. In gratitude, the Roman government granted the people of Cerveteri

the privilege of living in Rome without having to pay taxes or join the army. Later, it offered them partial citizenship.

But battles between Romans and Etruscans continued. In 356 BC, the Etruscans captured 307 Romans and sacrificed them to their gods in the main square of Tarquinia. The Romans fought back and conquered several cities, including Tarquinia and Cerveteri. Eventually, every Etruscan city became Roman, either by force or by alliance. Gradually, the two cultures intermingled, even though some Roman citizens proudly held to their Etruscan past.

Strangely enough, the Etruscan territories were considered a united region only after they became Roman, when Emperor Augustus named that area Etruria.

Cerveteri. Corinasdavide, Wikimedia Commons

ETRUSCAN ARCHITECTURE

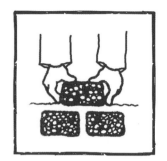

The Etruscans were creative and resourceful. They learned much from the Greeks but also made original discoveries. They developed a way to make strong **arches** for their buildings, bridges, and aqueducts—an invention often attributed to the Romans.

The arched gate of the Etruscan city of Volterra.
Sailko, Wikimedia Commons

The Etruscans also built an excellent road system and channeled water away from cities and into the fields. Their roads were built mostly with gravel and soil and were sometimes supported on the sides by blocks of tufa, which was common in the area and easy to cut and transport. On the sides or in the middle of the roads, the Etruscans dug channels to help drain rainwater. Later, the Romans perfected this system. Many Roman roads, such as the Via Cassia, were built over Etruscan roads. And according to the Romans, when the three Etruscan kings ruled Rome, they applied Etruscan knowledge of architecture and engineering to improve the city.

Houses and Cities

The early Etruscans lived in huts built with wood and mud bricks, topped by curved straw roofs. Several huts were usually built together to house extended families and store food. These homes were dark, with few windows, and with an opening on the roof to let out smoke from lamps, braziers, and fireplaces.

Build an Edible Etruscan Arch

Build an arch using only caramel candies. Although every block in an arch is equally important, you will see how important the top piece—which architects call the capstone or keystone—is in keeping the other pieces together.

Materials

11 caramel candies

1. Unwrap the candies. On a clean surface, make two stacks of two candies each. Press slightly to keep them in place. They will be your pillars.

2. Take the remaining seven candies and pinch each one on the bottom to create a trapezoid. The bottom portion should be about half the size of the top half.

3. Lay the seven pinched candies on the clean surface until they form an arch. Press them slightly together.

4. Pick up the arch and set it on the pillars you have built.

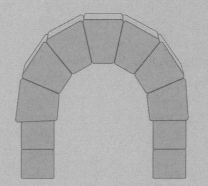

With time, the Etruscans began to build houses with bricks and painted them with bright colors. The floors were still clay, but the roofs were made with shingles. As in Rome, rich people decorated their homes with beautiful objects, paintings, and statues.

The Etruscans built most of their walled cities on hills so that guards could easily survey the surrounding lands and protect them from attacks. The temples and homes of rich people were built on the top of the hill, where they were safer, since enemies would typically raid the lower portion first—which included the city square, stores, workshops, other homes, and markets.

An Etruscan urn in the shape of a hut, originally made in Vulci around the eighth century bc. These urns were used to keep the ashes of people who had died. They give us a general idea of the homes of that time, with decorative designs on walls and roofs. On this urn, the ends of the poles on the roof are shaped to look like water fountains. Scala / Art Resource, NY

Sea towns like Tarquinia were built at a few miles' distance from the coast, to protect them from the frequent pirate raids. The only exception was Populonia, which was built directly across the island of Elba. The island was rich in metals, and it made sense to build a city nearby. Metal could be processed and shipped out without having to travel far.

Tombs

Initially, the Etruscans **cremated** their dead and placed the ashes in covered urns with personalized lids. Men's urns were often shaped like a helmet, and women's like a bowl. They were buried underground in well-like pits, along with objects the person had used in life.

As time passed, cremation became less common, and the burial places changed shape. They were often built inside a natural rock or

Interior of the Tomb of Reliefs in a necropolis at Cerveteri. Ekaterina Averina

TEMPLES

Early Etruscans might have worshiped in natural enclosures such as caves. They built their first temples around 600 BC, modeled on temples that Greeks had built in southern Italy. But Greek temples were built of marble or stone, and Etruscan temples were mostly built of wood and mudbricks, with clay tile roofs. Wood, mud, and clay don't last long, which is why Greek temples still exist but Etruscan temples do not.

Historians can describe Etruscan temples by studying ruins or the models or images found in tombs. The Roman Vitruvius also describes a "Tuscan temple" in his book on architecture.

Early Etruscan temples had multiple entrances, while later temples had only one entrance in front, emphasized by a brightly colored wall. Etruscan temples were built on a high podium. To reach the front door, visitors climbed a flight of stairs and walked through a covered patio surrounded by columns. Inside, there were usually three rooms, each built for a different divinity.

Etruscan temples built on the coast often faced the sea, as if they invited other populations to join in the worship. Three

bilingual golden tablets describing the dedication of a gift to the Phoenician goddess Astarte and her Etruscan equivalent, the goddess Uni, seem to confirm this idea of shared worship services.

A reconstruction of an Etruscan temple. Sailko, Wikimedia Commons

underground, covered with a large mound. Inside, they looked like real homes with rooms, except that all furniture was carved out of stone, including beds and pillows.

These burial places were grouped by family, inside of a walled space, as if they were homes inside a city. That's why historians don't call them cemeteries; they call them a necropolis, which means "city of the dead."

A necropolis was usually built outside the city walls. As a copy of the city itself, it often had streets, gutters, and homes. Because of this, archaeologists can deduce the appearance of Etruscan cities and homes.

Most of the tombs were carved from tufa, which could have yellow, gray, red, or green hues. Today, tufa is still extracted and shaped into blocks. The Etruscans cut it with hand tools for streets, homes, tombs, and temples.

ETRUSCAN CLOTHING

Like many other aspects of Etruscan culture, their fashion changed over time, from extremely simple attire meant to protect and keep them warm, to elaborate and varied fashion. Etruscans mostly used wool for their clothes, which could be made at home using a **spindle** to produce yarn and a **loom** to weave it.

Traditional stories say it was Tanaquil, wife of the first Etruscan king of Rome, who created the royal garments that became common in Roman ceremonies, such as the *tunica recta*. This garment is worn by brides before their weddings, and by boys before their official entrance into adulthood. Tanaquil might even have created the first gold trimmings for the purple togas of kings and the wedding gowns that became traditional for Roman women.

Those who could afford linen preferred it to wool, especially for inner clothing such as tunics—it was softer on the skin. Leather and fur were also popular. Wealthy people liked to show off exotic fur, often from wild African animals. Silk, a luxury from Eastern countries, was quite appreciated in Italy.

Like the Greeks (and later Romans), Etruscan men wore tunics as their basic clothing. It was sometimes short, above the knee. Most women's tunics went down to their feet and were often decorated with geometric patterns, stripes, flowers, stars, or polka dots. Sometimes they included golden borders and decorations—small roses, palms, or geometric figures. Tunics could be sleeveless or have short or long sleeves.

Over the tunics, some men wore a version of the toga, called a *tebenna*. There were no restrictions on who could wear this toga. Some

Tomb of Seianti Hanunia Tlesnasa. Her name is inscribed on her chest. She reclines on a mattress and pillow, holding a mirror in her left hand and raising her right hand to adjust her cloak. She wears a tunic with a high girdle, and many jewels: a tiara, earrings, a necklace, bracelets, and rings.
© The Trustees of the British Museum / Art Resource, NY

wore it without a tunic, leaving the right shoulder bare. Both men and women wore colorful cloaks, held in place with a **brooch**. Women could use the cloak to cover their heads.

Etruscan fashion differed from other nations' around them because, at least early on, Etruscan men and women often wore the same clothes. Some women wore a toga and a short tunic, like men. Some even wore their hair short.

Priests had their own style of clothing. They usually wore inside-out sheepskins over long tunics and cone hats held in place with chin straps.

Unlike Greeks and Romans, who used hats only for traveling or working in the fields, Etruscan men and women wore them often, and in many different shapes. Some hats were tall and round, others pointed, with or without a rim. The hats on some statues look like sombreros. Farmers wore smaller versions of this hat to protect them from the sun and rain.

Etruscans also had a variety of shoes, including sandals, over-shoes covered with bronze, and pointed-toe boots. Some sandals had wooden soles.

Cleanliness and Beauty

Etruscans cared about their appearance, which was a status symbol. Both men and women exercised and took care of their skin. Some used pitch to pull out unwanted body hair. Like the Romans and Greeks, they spread olive oil on their skin and scraped it off with a metal tool. They also used beauty masks. Mush made with ground-up barley, lentils, and narcissus bulbs, mixed with **resin**, eggs, and "Etruscan starch," was supposed to clear oily skin.

Etruscan women used a great variety of makeup and perfume. Their hair was braided, pulled up, or left flowing. One Etruscan statue shows a woman with a thin headband and multiple braids joined in a low ponytail in back.

Back side of an Etruscan bronze mirror, showing the legendary Greek seer Kalkas examining an animal liver.
Scala / Art Resource, NY

Some Etruscan men wore their hair long, sometimes braided. Some bleached their hair with a mixture of beech tree ashes and animal fats. Initially, men liked to grow beards and long hair. This fashion changed after the fifth century, when men followed the Greek fashion of short hair and shaved faces.

For adults who lost permanent teeth, Etruscan craftsmen made something close to today's partial dentures or bridges, which were removable or attached to the existing teeth. Craftsmen would either take some teeth from a person who had just died or carve them out of ox teeth. The new teeth were bound together with bands of gold that could rest on the patient's real teeth without touching the gums. Apparently, Etruscans didn't care if other people knew they were wearing false teeth. In fact, it might have been a sign of wealth, as poor people could not afford them.

Jewelry

Etruscans wore many jewels, as varied and creative as their clothes: bracelets, earrings, necklaces, **anklets**, rings, and small crowns.

Make an Etruscan Mirror

People have always liked to look at themselves, sometimes as a reflection in the waters of a lake or pond. Almost every ancient civilization created some type of mirror. Bronze mirrors were refined under the masterful hands of Etruscan and Celtic metalworkers. The backs of Etruscan mirrors were often decorated with images from everyday life, Greek mythology, or both.

Materials

Drawing compass (or an old CD)

2 7-inch dessert paper plates

Scissors

Plastic tablecloth or newspaper to protect working surfaces

Gold or bronze metallic acrylic paint

Paintbrush

1 6-inch jumbo popsicle stick

Black fine-point permanent marker

1 5-inch round mirror

Strong adhesive tape

Stapler

1. Place a compass in the center of a paper plate and draw a circle with a 2-inch radius.

2. Cut from the edge of the plate to the line you have drawn, then cut around the line.

3. Protect your workspace with a plastic tablecloth or newspaper.

4. Paint both sides of a popsicle stick and the white back side of both the cut plate and the second whole plate. Make sure the paint is spread evenly, especially on the whole paper plate. Let all the pieces dry. (Dry the popsicle stick propped up on the lid of the paint bottle.)

5. Wash your hands and paintbrush.

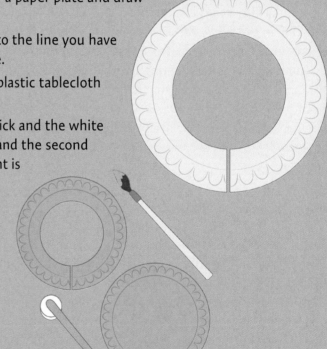

6. Once the plate is completely dry, use a marker to draw a picture of one or more famous characters on its back.

7. Place the cut paper plate right side up (as if using as a plate) on the table. Then place the mirror in the center of the plate, facing down. Use the tape to attach the mirror to the plate firmly.

8. Use more tape to ensure that the cut you made on the plate (from the edge to the line) is closed.

9. Use another piece of tape to attach the popsicle stick to the plate. About 2½ inches of stick should be outside of the plate. This will be the handle for your mirror.

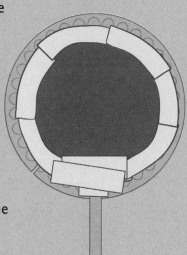

10. Place the decorated paper plate on top of the other, with the image up.

11. Staple the two plates together around the edges. Go slow and make sure the edges meet. Stapling close to the popsicle stick will reinforce the grip.

12. If needed, use clear tape to reinforce the handle.

13. Look at your image in the mirror. When you are tired of admiring yourself, turn the mirror around and relive your favorite story as the Etruscans did.

You may substitute the mirror by cutting a round shape from metallic card or heavy-duty aluminum foil. The view will not be clear, but neither was the Etruscans'.

Create an Elegant Etruscan Brooch

Etruscans wore different kinds of brooches. They were important because Etruscans had no buttons or zippers. This activity uses a technique similar to granulation to make an elegant gold brooch. You can use this brooch to keep a scarf in place for an Etruscan look.

Materials

Drawing compass

Small piece of cardboard

Scissors

1 piece of heavy-duty aluminum foil, 4 inches by 3 inches

White glue

Pencil

2-inch by 2-inch piece of paper

Clay-modeling tool

Silver duct tape (or other strong tape)

1 1¾-inch safety pin

Package of silver sugar pearls or small beads (sugar pearls are safest for younger kids)

Large scarf

1. Use a compass to draw a circle with a 2-inch diameter on a small piece of cardboard.

2. Use scissors to cut out the circle.

3. Lay a piece of aluminum foil on a table or other clean surface, shiny-side down.

4. Spread some glue evenly on one side of the circle.

5. Place the circle glue-side down on the aluminum foil. Stay close to one edge, without touching it completely.

6. Spread some glue evenly on the other side of the cardboard circle.

7. Fold the aluminum foil to cover the cardboard completely.

8. Cut the foil around the cardboard circle, without getting too close to the edges.

9. Smooth the edges of the foil so they cover the sides of the cardboard.

10. Draw a simple image on the small paper with a pencil—a flower, a sword, or a geometrical design.

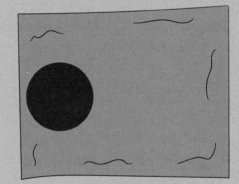

11. Place your drawing on the foil-covered side of the circle. Use the clay-modeling tool to gently trace the lines of the drawing. Lift the paper to make sure the lines are well marked on the foil.

12. Cut about 1 inch of silver duct tape and set it aside.

13. Turn your brooch over. Open the pin and place the clasp side against the middle of the circle. Hold the pin with one hand and tape the pin to the center of the circle.

14. Turn the brooch around again and place a little white glue in the lines you made.

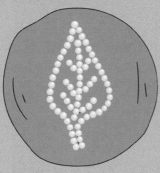

15. Gently place the silver pearls in the glue.

16. Allow the glue to dry completely.

17. Wear a scarf around your body any way you like—you may look at some pictures of Etruscan clothes for inspiration. Fasten it with the brooch you made.

Did this activity take time and concentration? Imagine attaching hundreds of tiny beads, much smaller than these.

Etruscan jewelers perfected ancient techniques to such a remarkable level that their works were in great demand all over the Mediterranean region.

They became experts in a technique called granulation—melting specks of gold or silver into tiny balls, which they later applied to a jewel or precious object. To accomplish this, they had to place the object in an oven hot enough to fuse the specks to the surface without melting them. This required impressive skills. Since Etruscans loved colors, their jewels often included precious stones or glass beads.

To many Romans, the Etruscans' colorful and expensive clothes, combined with their love of parties and extravagant tombs, showed that they were a wasteful and pampered people.

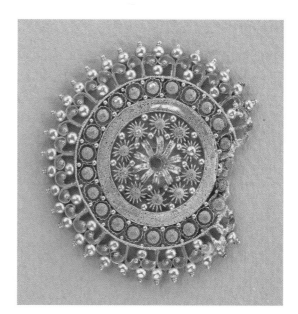

Etruscan gold brooch with granulation. The Etruscans knew how to attach to any surface balls that were less than $\frac{1}{200}$ inch in diameter. © RMN-Grand Palais / Art Resource, NY

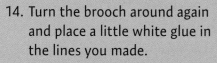

ETRUSCAN WRITING

Like the Romans and Greeks, the Etruscans wrote on tablets of wax or on papyrus. Some important documents were written on gold sheets, such as the three tablets relating a gift to the goddesses Astarte and Uni. These tablets are important because they are written in both Etruscan and Phoenician. They have been helpful to linguists, even though one text is not the translation of the other. Each side includes a different part of an agreement.

Most Etruscan writings that survive today were inscribed in stone, but they consist only of two or three words, usually names of people. Marke (today's Mark) was a common Etruscan name. The longest Etruscan text ever discovered (2,000 words) was written on cloth, which was later recycled to wrap an Egyptian mummy. It was apparently a calendar with instructions on how to bury the dead.

Etruscan characters were similar to those of the Greek alphabet, but the words were written from right to left. Etruscan didn't sound at all like other Mediterranean languages. For example, the phrase *Keliutis zatrumis flergva Netuns lesutri teter* (put into English letters) meant "On September 24, may the feast of Neptune be celebrated."

Like the Romans, Etruscans represented their numbers with symbols, which they combined in a similar way. For example, the symbol for 10 followed by the symbol for 1 (XI) meant 11. The numbers 1 and 10 were written exactly as they are in Roman numerals. Five,

though, was an upside-down V, 50 was an arrow pointing up, and 100 was a six-point asterisk. It made sense, because the bottom half of X (10) looks like an upside-down V and the bottom half of a six-point asterisk looks like an arrow pointing up.

For centuries, the Etruscan language was widely used and understood. Being highly cultured, Etruscans should have written some historical records, poems, letters, and stories. If they did, all these documents have disappeared. Because of this, many Etruscan mysteries have not yet been solved.

One of three golden tablets inscribed in the Etruscan language.
Universal Images Group / Art Resource, NY

Leave a Message on a Gold or Silver Tablet

Surprise a friend with a shiny card.

Materials

Blank greeting card

Heavy-duty gold or silver aluminum foil, a little larger than the card

Scissors

Foam board or mouse pad, same size as the card or larger

Scotch tape (optional)

Ballpoint pen

Piece of paper (optional)

1. Use a greeting card to measure a piece of aluminum foil to be slightly larger than the card on each side. Cut the piece and place it on the foam board or mouse pad. Make sure the foil is smooth, without wrinkles. If necessary, secure it with some scotch tape.

2. With the non-writing end of the ballpoint pen, write a short message on your piece of foil. (You can write the message on a piece of paper first so you can be sure it fits on the foil.)

3. Place the foil on the front of your greeting card and fold the edges around the card so that it fits smoothly.

4. Give it to a friend.

To make a fancier card, write the message backward in capital letters, from right to left, on a piece of paper. Stand in front of a mirror and check if your message reads correctly. If so, copy it as is on a piece of aluminum foil. Turn the foil around before attaching to the card and the letters will stand out.

Create a Secret Language

The Etruscan alphabet didn't have letters for our sounds b, d, and g. Instead, they substituted with p, t, and k. They also had only four vowels: a, e, i, and u. When Etruscans transcribed Roman names into their language, they spelled them differently. For example, Apollo, the Roman god of music, art, poetry, and medicine, was known in Etruria as Aplu. The Etruscan language was much more complex than this, but this activity can give you a general idea of some of its features. Try copying these patterns or make your own.

Materials

Pen or pencil

Paper

1. Write a sentence with a lot of *b*'s, *d*'s, or *g*'s. For example, "Dad doesn't give big dinners."

2. Now rewrite it, changing all the *b*'s, *d*'s, and *g*'s into *p*'s, *t*'s, and *k*'s respectively. The sentence above would become, "Tat toesn't kive pik tinners."

3. Now remove all the silent vowels and change the *o*'s into *u*'s. "Tat tusn't kiv pik tinners."

4. Starting from the right, write each letter backward to the left.

5. See if a friend can figure out what you originally meant to say.

ETRUSCAN ART AND MUSIC

Etruscans surrounded themselves with beautiful crafts and works of art. They learned much from other cultures (especially from the Greeks), but often surpassed their teachers, particularly in their sculptures. Sometimes, they took elements of Greek, Celtic, and Oriental art and developed original creations.

Paintings and Sculptures

The walls of some Etruscan tombs are decorated with impressive paintings and relief sculptures, which were carved partially into the stone. The paintings depict scenes of daily life, wild animals, and mythological heroes and creatures in red, light blue, yellow, green, black, and white.

The Tomb of Hunting and Fishing in Tarquinia shows a long seashore under an open sky, with colorful birds flying up and down, dolphins surging from the waves, a fishing boat, and a smiling diver. In another tomb, a common banquet is depicted in front of an open sea with a large **cargo** ship, and smaller ships in the background.

Since metals were abundant in Etruria, many Etruscan statues were made of bronze. In fact, when the Romans attacked the city of Volsinii (today's Orvieto) in 264 BC, they took away 2,000 bronze statues.

Detail of a wall painting in the Tomb of Hunting and Fishing at Tarquinia, Italy. Scala / Art Resource, NY

Making a bronze statue was a time-consuming task. The statue was made first from clay. It was then covered in beeswax, with attention to the smallest details, then covered with a mold of clay. A hole was left on top to pour in the bronze, and two holes on the bottom to drain the wax. Hot, liquid bronze was poured in through the top hole. It melted the wax and filled its place. Finally, the artist removed the mold and polished and refined the bronze statue.

Music

Music was important for the Etruscans—at meals, religious ceremonies, sports events, festivals, weddings, funerals, and even political occasions.

Paintings and archaeological findings show many different instruments, but the flute (called *aulos*) is the most common. The Greeks mostly associated the flute with Dionysus, god of wine, but the

Etruscans used it for many occasions of life and worship. Hunters carried the double flute to attract animals into their traps.

Some experts believe Etruscan double flutes were different from each other—one gave a single note, while the other gave a variety of sounds. The flutist held the second flute between the thumb and little finger, allowing the other fingers to move freely on the holes. Since there were five holes, however, it was probably played using two hands.

Trumpets were also common, either simple or curved, and were used especially in military operations and religious ceremonies. The

An Etruscan lid in the shape of an animal. It has a panther's head, but the body is curved to look almost like a weasel. The Walters Art Museum, Baltimore

This Etruscan bronze statue from the fifth or fourth century BC represents a mythological creature called Chimera (pronounced ky-MER-uh)—a fire-breathing lion with a serpent's tail and a goat head growing out of its back. Its hair stands up, showing both fear and readiness to attack. The inscription on one leg reads TINSCVIL (Gift to Tin), the head of the Etruscan gods. Album / Art Resource, NY

Give Your Backpack an Etruscan Handle

The Etruscans liked to be creative when making handles of any kind. Some had images of gymnasts doing a backbend or wrestlers fighting. Many were in the form of animals, which are common on many Etruscan objects.

Materials

Backpack or bag with handle

Small four-legged stuffed animal

String

1. Place a stuffed animal on the handle of your backpack so that the paws touch the two bottom sides of the handle.

2. Use a piece of string to fasten the back legs of the stuffed animal to one bottom side of the handle.

3. Use more string to fasten the front legs of the stuffed animal to the other side of the handle.

4. Use your newly improved backpack.

You can free your stuffed animal when you decide to give your backpack a different look.

POTTERY

The Etruscans made many vases in the typical Greek style—red vases with black pictures or black vases with red pictures—but they also invented something new. They found a way of baking **terra-cotta** so that it would come out black and shiny, looking like metal. (Terra-cotta clay was abundant in Etruria and could be used for both small and large sculptures, including coffin lids.) They called this invention bucchero (pronounced bukkero). The exact method was kept a secret. It was time consuming and required a special oven that couldn't be opened. Bucchero became extremely popular and fashionable all over the Mediterranean world.

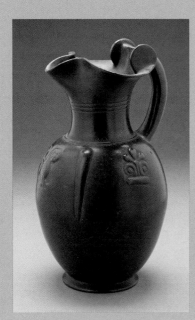

A sixth-century BC Etruscan jug in bucchero.
William Randolph Hearst Collection, Los Angeles County Museum of Art

A wall painting showing a musician playing a double flute. Scala / Art Resource, NY

curved trumpet, which ended in a coil, was similar to the Celtic *karnix* and was later adopted by the Romans.

The Etruscans also had string instruments similar to **lyres** (small U-shaped harps) and guitars, as well as percussion instruments, such as tambourines and castanets, called *crotales*. Etruscan *crotales* were usually made of two pieces of wood joined by a ring or string attached to the musician's wrist, allowing the musician to clap them together. On occasion, they used a rattle-like instrument called a *sistrum*, which was also used in Egyptian worship.

Etruscan instruments that have survived until today show they were made by expert and precise craftsmen. The flutes are perfect cylinders, with holes placed at the exact same distance in each instrument, all made without the help of modern tools.

ETRUSCAN RELIGION

The Etruscans worshiped many gods and goddesses. Initially, they worshiped them as spirits, without making any images. Not until the middle of the sixth century did they begin to portray them in statues or paintings, which resembled the Greek gods.

Tinia (or Tin), with his thunderbolt, is usually compared to the Greek Zeus and Roman Jupiter, though younger. His wife, Uni, corresponded to the Greek Era and Roman Juno, but she played a more important role. There were similar connections for the god of the seas,

Apollos (or Aplu) of Veii. Aplu, the god of prophecy, music, and youth, was an important god for the Etruscans, who gave a central place to prophecy. This terra-cotta statue is more dynamic than some Greek statues of the same time period. Scala/Ministero per i Beni e le Attività culturali / Art Resource, NY

Nethuns (the Greek Poseidon and Roman Neptune); the god of war, Maris (the Greek Ares and Roman Mars); and many more. There were also uniquely Etruscan divinities, such as Achvizr, Thalna, and Lasa Sitmica, who could be either male or female. Etruscans also worshiped the sun (Usil), the moon (Tiur), and the dawn (Thesan).

Etruscan gods were believed to control events of this life, but people believed they were able to influence them and even make them change their minds through sacrifices and offerings. Archaeologists have found some images of parts of the body that were related to the people's prayers. A person with an aching foot could offer a terra-cotta image of a foot to the gods to remind them what needed healing, or to express gratitude once the foot healed.

Etruscans believed there was a way to predict the gods' behavior, or to interpret the meaning of what they had done, by observing how birds flew or how chickens pecked their food, or by studying events, such as an unexpected rain shower or blooming flower. Trying to figure out what the gods know is called **divination**.

For the Etruscans, divination was a science and was practiced by trained priests and seers called **augures**, **fulguratores**, and **haruspices**. In general, augures believed they could tell the future by watching birds, fulguratores specialized in lightning, and haruspices deciphered divine messages by examining the insides of animals they sacrificed to the gods.

THE AFTERLIFE

There are no written descriptions of the Etruscans' beliefs about life after death, but the images in their tombs give a clear idea. The oldest images suggest that they believed in a happy underworld where people continued to enjoy the pleasures of this life. Yet these happy scenes could also represent the deceased's life on earth or the funeral ceremonies, which included banquets, games, and processions. Rich or influential families had especially elaborate ceremonies.

Funeral processions are often depicted in the tombs, showing long convoys of family members, public magistrates holding banners, musicians, and priests. There were also servants who carried the supplies to be left in the tombs.

Later in history, images on tomb walls gave greater emphasis to the trip the soul would take, led by demons such as Charun, who sailed the boat linking this world to the next, and Tuchulcha, a blue-skinned creature with wild hair, donkey ears, wings, and a vulture's beak, and by the goddess Vanth, who carried a torch, a scroll, a sword, and the keys of Hell.

Red-haired Charun, armed with a hammer to break down Hell's door, stands guard at a painted door in an Etruscan tomb, together with Vanth, who holds a torch. In spite of their scary appearances, their jobs were not to punish the dead but to escort them to the underworld. Painted doors were common inside of tombs as a symbol to the way to the underworld. © DeA Picture Library / Art Resource, NY

There was also a three-headed sea dragon, Idra, who terrified the dead as they traveled to the next life. If anyone cut off one of its heads, two would grow in its place. According to Etruscan mythology, Hercle (the Roman hero Hercules) was finally able to kill Idra.

Bronze model of a sheep's liver. It helped the Etruscan haruspices predict the future. Scala / Art Resource, NY

The most important organ for divination was the liver. Each portion of the liver had a particular meaning. Etruscan seers engraved the instructions for this type of divination in a life-size bronze model of a sheep liver, which includes the names of 21 Etruscan gods and goddesses.

Divination followed exact rules that were included in the *Tagetic Books*. According to Etruscan tradition, it all started when a farmer named Tarcontes was surprised by a sudden apparition while plowing a field. The spiritual being looked like an old man and a child at the same time. He emerged from the ground and introduced himself as Tagetes, then asked Tarcontes to write down what he was about to reveal: the laws of divination. Tarcontes carefully recorded every one of Tagetes's words. Then Tagetes disappeared, leaving Tarcontes with the precious *Tagetic Books*.

Etruscans consulted augures and haruspices before making important decisions. They even asked their gods to reveal when, where, and how they should build their cities. They believed their civilization would only last 10 "ages." These ages were not composed of a specific number of years. Instead, the end of each age was marked by a major event and acknowledged by the haruspices.

The haruspices believed a prophecy marked the end of the eighth age. They declared the beginning of the 10th and final age at the time of Augustus. In reality, by the time Augustus became emperor, the Etruscan civilization had already been absorbed into Roman culture. But in some ways it never truly ended, as its art, culture, and religion continued. When the Goth Alaric started his march against Rome in AD 408, the haruspices offered to save the town by observing the insides of animals—as they claimed to have done in a nearby town called Narnia. Both the city ruler and the pope agreed, but the haruspices demanded all senators participate, and they refused.

ETRUSCAN GOVERNMENT AND WARFARE

Etruscan cities were originally independent, each with its own laws and its own ruler, called a *lucumone*. Lucumones came from rich and powerful families and ruled until they died. They wore a purple tunic and a crown and held a scepter, usually topped with a bronze eagle, the symbol of royalty.

Lucumones made new laws, commanded the army, and oversaw religious rites. This triple power was symbolized with an ax wrapped in a bundle of sticks. The sticks represented the power of the judge, who used rods to punish lawbreakers, and the army. The ax represented religious power, because axes were used in temples to sacrifice animals to the gods. The bundle was also a symbol of unity, because a bundle of sticks is stronger than individual ones.

The same symbol was later adopted by the Romans, who called it fasces. Fasces were carried by special officers called lictors, who escorted men of power. In 20th-century Italy, this became the symbol of fascism, a form of dictatorial government. It still appears in US courts of law, and on the back of US dimes.

Even though the Etruscans never formed a single state, they were united by common language, religion, and customs. Sometimes the cities joined for military, financial, or religious reasons—to fight an enemy, to import or export goods, or to hold a religious festival.

Initially the Etruscans, either alone or in alliance with other populations, won a few victories over the Romans. In the end, however, they couldn't stop the force of the highly disciplined Roman army. One reason the Etruscan civilization fell might be that Rome was united, while the Etruscan cities were all self-governing and often warred against each other.

Etruscan or Roman fasces on the back of a 1916 US dime, known as a Mercury Dime. This coin was minted before fascism came to power in Italy and is not connected to it.
BrandonBigheart, Wikimedia Commons

ETRUSCAN DAILY LIFE

Much about the Etruscans' daily life can be learned by observing their tombs. The fact that they built family tombs for their immediate and extended families and their descendants shows that they thought family was very important. Since men and women are often depicted together during banquets and processions, and sculpted together on their tombs, historians believe Etruscan women enjoyed a higher status than women in Greek or Roman society. This is also supported by the fact that, initially, women had their own names instead of feminine versions of their fathers' names, as was the Roman custom. Some Etruscan names for women were Tanaquil, Ramtha, Thania, Hathli, Pevtha, Sethra, and Thanusa.

This custom changed when Rome began exercising greater influence over Etruria. Some images changed too. For example, while the men were depicted holding special cups used in religious rituals, the women with them held fans or pomegranates, giving the impression that they were excluded from some religious ceremonies.

Greek and Roman authors didn't approve of the place Etruscan women held in their society. They thought the Etruscan habits of

This terra-cotta lid for an Etruscan tomb shows a husband and wife smiling together. Placing a husband and wife together on a tomb was uniquely Etruscan and has led experts to believe that Etruscan women were more respected than other women of their time.
© RMN Grand Palais / Art Resource, NY

allowing women to mingle with men in sports activities and at parties, instead of keeping them with other women or with their husbands, were scandalous and dangerous. They even depicted the Etruscan women as immoral. But Greek and Roman writers often exaggerated descriptions of the unconventional behaviors of other populations, mostly to show the contrast with the moderate and virtuous customs of Rome. It's wise to take their words with a grain of salt, not judge an entire nation on the words of outsiders.

In any case, Etruscan women were expected to perform the usual feminine tasks of raising children, spinning wool, and weaving clothes. Unless they were rich enough to afford servants, they took care of the house and the cooking.

Spinning and weaving were considered noble activities even for richer women, who did them while supervising the work of their slaves. Creating a simple piece of cloth took time. Historians have calculated that 5-by-15 feet of linen cloth would have taken one person 650 hours to produce—575 hours to spin the yarn and 75 to weave it. For one person, this could be more than 80 eight-hour days! Because of this, the work was usually divided among many people. Weaving was usually done in groups of two. Also, portable spindles allowed women to spin yarn while walking or doing other activities that didn't involve their hands.

The Etruscans at Work

Many Etruscans were farmers, fishermen, merchants, and artisans (working mostly in metal and clay). There were also engineers and builders who created tombs, homes, temples, aqueducts, ships, and chariots, as well as workers who produced the raw materials. Tomb images also show entertainers, such as musicians, dancers, tightrope walkers, and jugglers.

Mining was the worst job of all. It was important, because many essential objects were made of metal, but it was also dangerous and caused health problems. It was usually left to slaves, most of whom were prisoners of war. Some of the wealthiest Etruscans became rich from trading goods and from directing the work at the mines. Their tombs show luxury objects common people could never afford.

Fun and Games

Etruscans played many sports, such as relay races, boxing, long jump, pole-vault, wrestling, and discus and javelin throw. People also enjoyed chariot races, which were held in special arenas outside the city or near sacred areas, and horse races, which occurred inside labyrinths. Some games were performed in honor of the dead during funeral celebrations.

Gladiator matches, which were extremely popular in Rome, were probably an Etruscan invention. As in Rome, many of these games ended with the death of one fighter. Sometimes they were used to execute criminals or prisoners of war, who had to fight with their heads covered by a large hood so they could not see their opponents. In this, Etruscans were just as cruel as Romans.

They also liked to fish and hunt, not only for food but also for sport. One of their favorite hunting preys was wild boar, considered a demonic creature to be destroyed.

At home, people played dice and board games similar to checkers or backgammon. Children shared the same toys as their peers in Rome and Greece: tops, walnuts, knucklebones, and so on.

Build an Etruscan Dodecahedron

Etruscans used regular six-sided dice like those sold today, but they also used other shapes.
Archaeologists have found an Etruscan dodecahedron, a solid geometrical figure with 12 sides.
A dodecahedron allows you to have more options when you play.

Materials

Internet access

Printer

Sheet of thick, heavy paper

Colored pencils or crayons

Black marker

Scissors

Glue stick

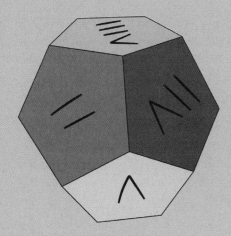

1. Go to: https://commons.wikimedia.org/wiki/File:Foldable_dodecahedron_(blank).jpg.

2. Select "Original File."

3. Load a sheet of paper in the printer and print the image. Under layout, choose "Landscape." Heavy card stock paper works well.

4. Color the 12 identical shapes (pentagons) in the design.

5. With the black marker, write the Etruscan numbers from 1 to 12 on the pentagons: I, II, III, IIII, V, VI, VII, VIII, VIIII, X, XI, XII.

6. Cut out the figure, including the little tabs, paying special attention to the small spaces.

7. Fold the figure along each line, pressing hard to mark the creases.

8. Join the pentagons, one by one, by spreading a little glue on every small tab and placing the tab under the next pentagon. Press firmly as you join them. You may have to use a little extra glue on the last two tabs.

9. Stop occasionally and wait for the glue to dry.

10. Use the dodecahedron to play any game that requires two dice.

ETRUSCAN FOOD

Etruscans liked to eat. Being good fishers and hunters, they ate a lot of fish and venison—wild boar, hares, deer, and game birds. From the abundant woods, they picked chestnuts, berries, and acorns (for the pigs).

Farmers raised sheep, goats, cows, pigs, and chickens. They also grew fruits and vegetables, nuts, olives, grains, lentils, and chickpeas, and made cheese and wine. Eggs were important not only in the daily diet but also as symbols of fertility and life. Archaeologists have found egg shells in many tombs, probably leftovers from funerary banquets.

Like the Greeks and Romans, Etruscans raised a small animal called a dormouse (similar to a squirrel), which they considered a delicacy. They kept the dormice on separate shelves in special clay pots with holes until they were ready to eat them. Food was flavored with herbs, pepper, other spices, honey, and vinegar. Honey was a favorite ingredient. Sometimes Etruscans even added it to wine.

In the Greco-Roman world, Etruscans had a reputation of being fat. This is possible, given the abundance of food in their region and their lavish parties. Some Etruscan statues have big bellies. At the same time, it could have been one of the stereotypes Greeks and Romans used to claim Etruscans were lazy and spoiled, lacking the strict and moderate behavior that was considered of great value in Greece and Rome.

RECLINING ETRUSCANS

Etruscans ate most meals sitting down. During special dinners, however, they moved to a specific room furnished with dining couches, resting one arm on cushions and using the other arm to reach for food and eat.

Have you ever eaten while lying on your side? Is it comfortable? What are the advantages of eating in this position? What are the disadvantages?

Warm Up with a Bowl of Etruscan Soup

Unlike the Romans, the Etruscans didn't leave any cookbooks. Historians try to understand what the Etruscans ate by looking at tomb paintings of people eating or preparing food, and utensils and scraps of food found in the necropolis. They have found wine vessels, pestles, braziers, pots of all sizes, cutting boards, rolling pins, cheese graters, chickpeas, egg shells, and bones. Some historians have matched these findings with traditional Italian recipes from Etruscan areas, recipes that might have passed from generation to generation. One of these is the Tuscan **acquacotta**, *a soup made with bread, vegetables, and eggs. This recipe uses dandelion greens because they grow in the wild, as they probably did in Etruscan times. It also uses pita bread because flatbreads were also common.*

ADULT SUPERVISION REQUIRED

Materials

½ bunch of dandelion greens (or other leafy green vegetable)

½ onion

1 clove of garlic

Cutting board

Knife

Small pot with lid

2 tablespoons of olive oil

¼ carrot, ¼ stalk of celery, and/or ¼ zucchini (optional)

2 cups of water

Bowl

Pita bread, flatbread, crackers, or toasted French bread

1 tablespoon of grated Romano cheese

1 egg

Salt

1. Wash the dandelion greens. Peel the onion and the clove of garlic.
2. Place the onion and garlic on the cutting board and, with an adult's help, chop them finely. If you use a carrot, celery, and/or zucchini, chop them too.
3. Cut the greens into small pieces.
4. Pour the oil into the pot. Add the chopped vegetables and ask an adult to cook them until golden.
5. Add the water to the pot. Have an adult heat until boiling.
6. When the water is boiling, add the dandelion greens and let them cook.
7. Break the bread into small pieces and place them inside the bowl. Sprinkle the cheese on top.
8. Remove the pot from the heat. Gently crack the egg into it without breaking the yolk.
9. Place the pot on the fire again, cover it with the lid, and let it cook until the egg is poached (ask an adult to check).
10. Pour the soup into the bowl on top of the bread.
11. Taste the soup and add salt as needed. (Romano cheese is naturally salty.)

PART III: THE CELTS

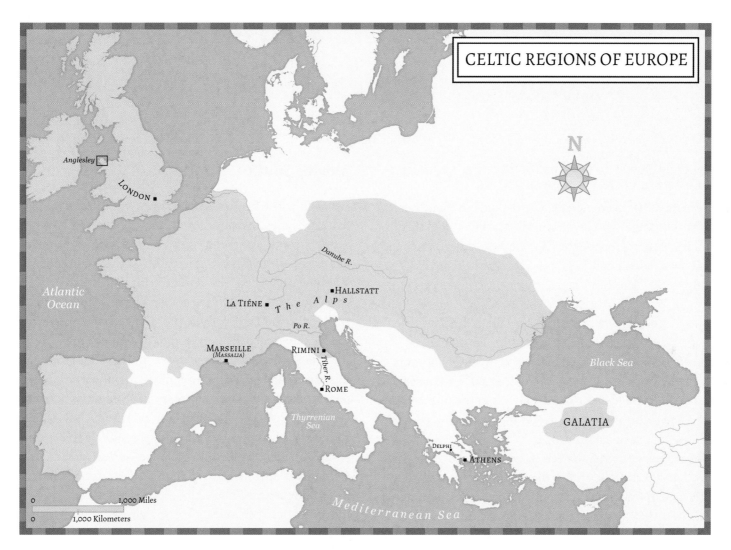

CELTIC REGIONS OF EUROPE

N

Anglesley

LONDON

Atlantic Ocean

Danube R.

■HALLSTATT

LA TIÉNE ■ The Alps

Po R.

MARSEILLE
(MASSALIA)

RIMINI ■
Tiber R.

■ROME

Thyrrenian Sea

Black Sea

GALATIA

DELPHI
■ATHENS

Mediterranean Sea

0   1,000 Miles
0   1,000 Kilometers

The Celts in Europe

CELTIC HISTORY

Both Greeks and Romans wrote about a fierce European population with frightening looks, strange habits, and a terrifying army. In reality, they were not a single people but many tribes who shared similar languages and customs. The Greeks called them *Keltoi*. The Romans, who first encountered them in northern Italy and France, called them *Galli* (in English, Gauls). Today, the word *Celts* is used generically while *Gauls* describes the ancient populations of France.

No one knows for certain where the Celts originated. Some large cemeteries found in Hallstatt, Austria, and La Tène, Switzerland, belonged to Celtic populations. In fact, for centuries historians thought these were the original locations of the Celts. They believed that the Hallstatt civilization lasted from the eighth to the fifth century BC, when the La Tène civilization started, and that the Celts spread from those areas to other regions of Europe.

In reality, other groups of Celts thrived in early Europe, especially in Spain and northern Italy, and Celtic languages were spoken along the Atlantic Ocean (including parts of Portugal, Spain, France, Scotland, Ireland, and Wales), suggesting that much Celtic culture may have spread through trade and travel. But no one knows if all the people called Celts were related or simply shared a similar culture. Historians use that name for convenience.

Moving South

According to Roman historian Livy, around 600 BC a group of Celts led by King Bellovesus moved into Italy to find new lands. They settled in a large territory between the Alps and the Po River. Historians now believe other Celtic tribes had settled there much earlier.

Inevitably, the Celts clashed with the Etruscans and other populations. In 390 BC, a band of soldiers from a Celtic tribe called Senones traveled to the Etruscan town of Clusium to conquer it. Frightened, the local people called on Rome (100 miles north) for help.

The Romans sent three peace ambassadors to speak with Brennus, the Senones' leader. Brennus laid out his conditions: to maintain peace, Clusium would have to give the Senones some territory. He thought it was fair, since Clusium had land to spare, and besides, Rome had constantly taken land from the people around them.

Arguments turned into violence, and a Roman ended up killing a Celtic warrior. The Celts then turned in fury against the Romans, who fled on horseback. The Celts sent a group of envoys to Rome, asking for justice. When the Romans refused, the Celtic army marched toward Rome.

The Romans met the Celts 11 miles north of Rome near the River Allia, a small **tributary** of the Tiber. Their general, Quintus Sulpicius, warned his men that the Celts were more dangerous than the Italian populations they had been battling. According to the Greek historian Diodorus Siculus, the Celts looked terrifying. They were tall, "with rippling muscles," deep and harsh voices, and blond hair. Their military tactics were also different. They counted on their fearsome appearance, loud trumpets, and weapons to scare the enemy from the start.

In the end, the Romans took flight. Some were killed while fleeing, and others drowned in the Allia, weighed down by their armor. Only a few reached Rome, throwing the city into panic. Preparing for the worst, the Romans gathered their able-bodied men atop a fortified area of town called Capitoline Hill, while the women, children, and older men found refuge in the countryside.

According to tradition, Roman senators stayed in their homes, where they sat perfectly still, like statues. The city looked empty. When a surprised Celt pulled the beard of one of the "statues," the Roman hit him on the head with his staff. The Celt then killed the man and the other soldiers attacked the remaining senators.

The Celts waited outside the walls of Capitoline Hill, thinking the Romans wouldn't last long without supplies. After a few days, they launched a surprise attack, but their footsteps were heard by a band of geese. The birds cackled so loudly the Romans woke up to defend their position.

It was a small victory for the Romans, but they eventually had to give up. Thankfully, the Celts were only interested in riches. They didn't want to take over Rome, which they thought was insignificant. They demanded 1,000 pounds in gold, an enormous price for a looted city. When someone objected that the Celts used false weights, Brennus put his sword on the scale and said, "Woe to the conquered." The defeated Romans were completely at his mercy.

Whether these stories are true or exaggerated, the Romans had to admit defeat. In spite of their financial losses, they eventually

recovered and rebuilt, adding a powerful stone wall around the city for protection. This was the last foreign invasion of Rome until AD 410.

About a century later, a huge army of Celts marched from north of the Danube River all the way to Greece, where they were defeated and forced to retreat. Some Celts then settled in a region of today's Turkey, where they became known as "Galatians."

Julius Caesar and the Defeat of Gaul

Tensions between Celts and Romans continued for centuries, but the Romans kept the Celts out of Roman territories. The Romans placed three military **colonies** in northern Italy and extended one of their main roads, the Via Flaminia, to Ariminum (today's Rimini), so that troops could quickly march to the Celtic territories below the Alps.

Many Celtic tribes resented this control. When the Carthaginian general Hannibal Barca crossed the Alps to attack Rome in 218 BC, some Celtic tribes sided with him. They were a great help, supplying provisions, warriors, and information. Being skilled horsemen, the Celts were especially valuable in battle, contributing to Hannibal's astounding victories.

With time, the region became increasingly Romanized and gained the name Gallia Togata (Gaul with togas). Some citizens continued to resist the Roman rule. In 73 BC, some sided with the slave Spartacus in his rebellion against Rome.

In the meantime, beyond the Alps, Celtic and Germanic tribes kept fighting against each other. In 123 BC, the seaport of Massalia (today's Marseille) asked the Romans for protection against invaders. The Romans agreed in exchange for a strip of land to build a road to Spain. In 121 BC, this strip became the first Roman province outside Italy. The Romans called it Provincia Nostra (Our Province). Part of this territory became the modern French region of Provence.

In 58 BC, Julius Caesar became governor of this area. He saw the constant battles between Celts as an excuse to take over more of their land and started a six-year war. Caesar largely won. His troops were better equipped and trained. The Gauls fought hard and impressed Caesar with their clever ideas. At the end of the war, he wrote a book about their armies and their way of life, which is still useful to historians.

The main weakness of the Gauls was that they were not united as one people. But a 30-year-old nobleman named Vercingetorix finally succeeded in uniting their forces. After traveling around the country to meet tribal leaders, he created a federation of tribes to defeat the Romans. They weakened the enemy with short, surprise attacks and cut off Roman supply and communication lines.

In the summer of 52 BC, after a short battle against the Romans, Vercingetorix retreated with his forces into the town of Alesia. He was confident of victory, because Alesia was well fortified, on top of a steep hill. Before Caesar could react, Vercingetorix asked other tribes for reinforcements. Caesar understood Vercingetorix's plan and ordered his troops to build two huge walls, as well as ditches and traps, to block other armies from entering Alesia, or Vercingetorix from leaving.

Finally, Vercingetorix's reinforcements arrived. According to Caesar, there were 250,000 soldiers and 8,000 horsemen. Finding a weak spot in the Roman fortifications, the armies attacked. It was a tough battle. In the end, the Romans succeeded and Vercingetorix was forced to surrender, casting his weapons and armor at Caesar's feet.

Caesar sent Vercingetorix to Rome as prisoner. Six years later, he paraded him through the streets of Rome, then had him killed.

The Conquest of Britain

During these wars against the Gauls, Caesar led his troops twice to Britain, where the local tribes spoke a Celtic language and shared

No one knows what Vercingetorix looked like. This statue was created in the 19th century by French sculptor Aimé Millet, who showed Vercingetorix as a national hero. Jochen Jahnke at German Wikipedia

traditions with the Gauls. Caesar's first raid in 55 BC was largely unsuccessful. The following year, he installed a new tribal king, Mandubracius, who was friendly to Rome. Caesar realized a full conquest of Britain was not worth the effort.

Augustus continued Caesar's policy, and Rome continued to have good relations with Britain. British tribes were eager to trade with Rome, and the occasional problems were resolved through **diplomacy** rather than force.

Emperor Claudius sent 40,000 Roman troops to Britain in AD 43. Most historians believe that Claudius sought a conquest because his "approval ratings" in Rome were low. Taking advantage of a local rebellion, he staged an all-out invasion of the country.

The leader of the rebellion, Caractacus, fought for eight years until he was betrayed by another tribe. Claudius spared the lives of Caractacus and his family. The Roman historian Tacitus said that Caractacus earned his forgiveness by giving a moving speech in the Roman Senate, proclaiming Rome's glory.

By this time, Romans' opinions of the Celts were divided. Some thought they were barbarians who fought impulsively, drank too much wine, and offered human sacrifices to their gods. Others admired their virtues and courage, which Romans seemed to have lost. Tacitus wrote that the Romans—with all their luxury and self-indulgence—had corrupted the Celts. The truth probably lies somewhere in between, and Celts and Romans learned a lot from each other.

In AD 60, rebel tribes joined for one major attack against the Romans. Their leader was Boudicca, queen of the Iceni. Her husband, Prasutagus, had had good relations with the Romans, but after his death Roman armies invaded and plundered Boudicca's territories, beat her with a whip, and assaulted her daughters.

In revenge Boudicca, her warriors, and troops from neighboring tribes fought with a fury the Romans had never expected. They burned two cities to the ground, including Londinium (today's London), and killed tens of thousands of Romans. It was the most serious rebellion the Romans had ever faced in Britain.

Boudicca frightened the Roman army. Roman historian Cassius Dio described her as "very tall, in appearance most terrifying, in the glance of her eye most fierce, and her voice was harsh; a great mass of the tawniest [red] hair fell to her hips; around her neck was a large golden necklace; and she wore a tunic of [different] colors over which a thick mantle was fastened with a brooch."

Eventually, the Romans defeated the Celts in a disastrous battle. They were still outnumbered, but they had superior training and equipment. Boudicca died soon after the end of the battle. Some historians say she died of disease; others say she poisoned herself rather than submit to the Romans.

Eventually, Rome sent better governors to Britain and peace returned. Scotland, however, was still free from Roman influence. In AD 122, Emperor Hadrian ordered a wall built to mark the border between Roman Britain and Scotland. It was an impressive 80-mile wall, the greatest structure the Roman army had ever erected. It was meant to give the Scottish Celts the message that Rome was there to stay. Twenty years later, the Romans pushed the border farther north, when Emperor Antoninus Pius commissioned the building of the 40-mile-long Antonine Wall.

Since the Celts were not united, it's hard to trace their history beyond their relations with Rome. After Britain became part of the Roman Empire, most Celts absorbed the culture of Rome, although many elements of their culture and language have survived to this day.

A statue of Boudicca and her daughters on a chariot, created by British sculptor Thomas Thornycroft. Like other Celtic warriors, she is portrayed as a national heroine. Lily15, Wikimedia Commons

CELTIC ARCHITECTURE

The ancient Celts built few structures that still stand. We know about their homes and villages from writings by Greeks and Romans who visited Celtic lands. Ditches of some fortified Celtic villages can still be seen from the air, even though the buildings have been destroyed.

Homes

Initially, most Celts built their homes with a mixture of wooden poles and flexible tree branches. The homes were usually rectangular, except in Britain, where they were often round. The Celts daubed the walls with a mixture of clay and vegetable fibers, which hardened as it dried. The roof was made the same way.

Recent reconstructions have shown that Celtic houses were warm and dry, even in northern areas where the climate was much harsher than the conditions Romans and Etruscans experienced in Italy. Some homes in the far north were made of stone or a combination of wood and stone.

Celtic homes had large doors but no windows. Inside was just one large room, with a central stone hearth for warmth and cooking. A horizontal pole held a **cauldron** over the fire. Smoke escaped through a hole left open in the roof, though much of it stayed inside.

The Celtic hillfort of Uffington Castle, Berkshire, England, was built on these foundations around the eighth or seventh century BC. Tyler Bell, Wikimedia Commons

Celtic roundhouses, reconstructed from archaeological findings at Castel Henllys, Wales. Keith Ruffles, Wikimedia Commons

Mousa Broch, in Scotland is the best-preserved broch in the world. It was probably built around 100 BC. Langus, Wikimedia Commons

Some homes had an upper **loft** for sleeping and an underground room to store grain. The storage room was lined with stone and sealed with clay to keep out air, moisture, and rats. Archaeologists have tested this system and found it works well. Beds were simple mattresses filled with wool and covered with wool or fur blankets. Families kept animals inside at night, making the home even warmer.

In Scotland, archaeologists have found the remains of unique round homes called "wheel-houses," because the inside walls were built like the spokes of a wheel, with rooms in between.

Another type of ancient Scottish building is called the broch, a tall tower with double walls and a large inside space. Some historians believe they were used as fortresses, but in that case, why were they so tall? And if more than one family lived inside, it would have been cramped. Other experts believe they were built to store grain, or were fortified homes for prestigious wealthy families, like castles.

Celtic Villages

Many Celtic villages were built on hills and protected by strong walls. Around the fifth or sixth century BC, some of these fortified centers developed into cities, with a royal residence and shops. The Romans called them *oppida*.

Julius Caesar was impressed by the strength of the walls that surrounded some Gallic cities. The Gauls, he said, would place large wooden beams on the ground, two feet from each other. The ends of the beams would become part of the stone walls. Between the beams, Gauls would pour cement and soil. They continued to build the wall, adding beams, though the wooden beams never touched each other.

Build an Edible Gallic Wall

You can get a general idea of how Gauls built their walls by constructing one you can eat later.

Materials

Cutting board

Butter knife

30 Rice Krispy Treats

Plate

13 Italian biscotti

Tray

Box of dry cereal

1. On a cutting board, cut 30 Rice Krispy Treats in half lengthwise.

2. Line four biscotti on a tray so that they are parallel to the short sides of the tray.

3. Place one treat between the ends of two biscotti. Do the same at the other end. Repeat with the other biscotti. Press gently so that the treats are as close as possible to the biscotti.

4. Starting from the left, build another layer of treats and biscotti similar to the first. The corner treat should be perpendicular to the lower biscotti wall; then place one biscotti going across the lower treat wall. Alternate treats parallel to the first treat layer and perpendicular biscotti supports. This layer will include only three biscotti.

5. Use treats to fill the spaces between the biscotti ends on the opposite side.

6. Build a full layer of treats on top of the two biscotti on the two short sides.

7. Create a third layer all around. Use only treats on the short sides and alternate biscotti and treats on the long sides. This time, you might want to start building from the right. The important thing is that the biscotti don't lay on top of one another.

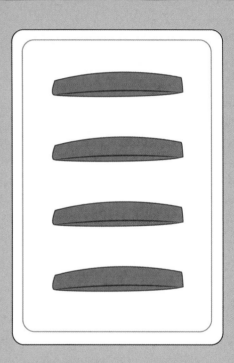

8. Do the same for a fourth layer.

9. End with a layer of treats only.

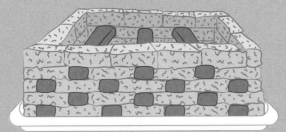

10. Pour cereal into the middle of your wall, making sure it falls between the biscotti. The Gauls used soil and clay for this.

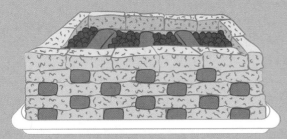

A Rice Krispy wall will not protect a city, but it will give you a hands-on understanding of how the Gauls built their walls.

The final wall was so strong that weapons of that day could not destroy it. "The stone protects it from fire, and the wood from the **battering ram**," Caesar wrote.

To enter these fortified cities, Caesar had to build wooden structures that allowed his soldiers to climb over the walls, but this was a difficult and dangerous method.

Ruins of an original Gallic wall (partially reconstructed) at Sermuz, Switzerland. Christos Nüssli (Euratlas), Wikimedia Commons

CELTIC CLOTHING

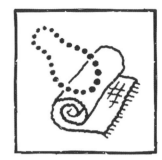

Since the Celts were spread over a wide territory, their clothes varied. Overall, they looked "striking" to travelers like the Greek Diodorus, who visited different Celtic regions. Both men and women wore tunics that were generally shorter than those worn by Roman and Greeks and tied around the waist with a belt. Men also wore pants, and women long skirts. Over this, they wore cloaks held together with iron or bronze brooches. These cloaks were "heavy for winter wear and light for summer."

Celtic brooches could be simple, such as a long, straight pin, or elaborate and creative. Some were shaped like animals, often horses, which, being very expensive, were a symbol of status and power. Many brooches included colorful stones, glass, or coral. Some experts believe brooches might have been used as **talismans** to ward off evil and bring good fortune.

Celtic brooch, from about 600 BC. Gift of J. Pierpont Morgan, 1917, to the Metropolitan Museum of Art, NY

CELTIC BEAUTY

Celtic women wore their hair long, braided, or pulled up. Men's hair could be long or short and usually was combed back. According to Diodorus, "Some of them shave the beard, but others let it grow a little; and the nobles shave their cheeks, but they let the mustache grow until it covers the mouth." Diodorus didn't think growing mustaches was a clean habit. "When they are eating," he said, "their mustaches become entangled in the food, and when they are drinking, the beverage passes, as it were, through a kind of a strainer."

Not all Celts were blond and tall. Those who lived in northern Europe were generally taller and had lighter hair than the people of the south. The men must have liked blond hair, because some lightened it using a mixture of powdered **limestone** and water. This chalky, white mixture produced stiff and coarse spikes, which made Celts look all the more fearful to their Mediterranean enemies.

According to another Greek writer, Strabo, the Celts detested being fat and punished any young man who went over "the standard measure of the girdle."

Create a Celtic Brooch

Many Celtic brooches were made by twisting strings of metal into imaginative designs. One end of the string was usually turned to form a pin. Try this technique in making your own brooch.

Materials

Silver or gold pipe cleaner

Loosely knit scarf

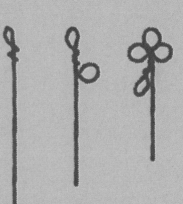

1. Bend back one end of a pipe cleaner about 1½ inches from the end, to make a loop. Twist the loop twice to close it, as shown.

2. Bend the pipe cleaner again at about 1½ inches from the end of the loop and wrap it around your fingertip to create a small circle.

3. Repeat two more times. This will create three circles.

4. Push the top of each circle inward slightly to make the figure look like a clover.

5. Twist the loose end of the pipe cleaner around the end of the clover to secure it.

6. Insert the loose end of the pipe cleaner through the stitches of the scarf, joining two sides together.

7. Now insert the loose end of the pipe cleaner through the hoop and press to secure it.

Enjoy the brooch as it keeps your scarf in place.
You can use the same method to make other designs: a single heart, a small heart inside a large one, a flower, or an abstract figure.

Weave a Colorful Mat

Celtic looms were made of wood and had iron weights to keep the threads in place.
This activity uses a simple cardboard box to give you an idea of basic weaving.

Materials

Empty rectangular tissue box

Scissors

Scotch tape

Ruler

Pen or marker

Tack

2⅛-inch plastic sewing needle

Skein of multicolored yarn (or yarn scraps from other projects)

Fork

1. Use scissors to cut off the top of the box.

2. Reinforce the sides of the box with tape, especially near the top.

3. Using a ruler, measure 1 inch from the top on one of the short sides of the box, close to one edge. Make a mark with the pen or marker.

4. Do the same farther down on the same side, close to the other edge. Draw a line to join the two marks. Mark this side of the box with an A.

5. Repeat steps 3 and 4 for the other short side of the box. Mark this side of the box with a B.

6. Position the ruler back on the first line you drew (on side A), and make ½-inch marks from one end to the other.

7. Do the same on side B.

8. Punch holes through all your pen marks, using a tack. Wiggle the tack to widen the holes. Be careful—watch your fingers!

9. Thread yarn onto a needle. Cut a long piece and secure the end with a knot.

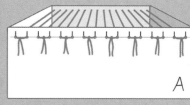

10. Use the needle to run the yarn through the first hole on side A of the box and then through the corresponding hole on side B.

11. Push the needle through the next hole on side B, running it all the way through the corresponding hole on side A. Pull the two ends on side A so that they are even, and tie them together with a loose knot (you will undo it later).

12. Repeat steps 9–11, filling all the holes until you reach the last one.

13. Thread the yarn onto the needle again. Cut another piece, as long as you think you can manage. You will need a lot of yarn to do the weaving. Secure the end of the yarn with a knot.

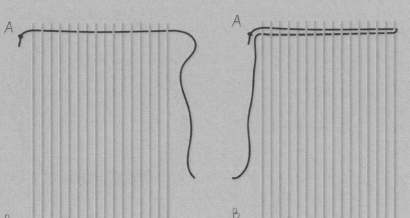
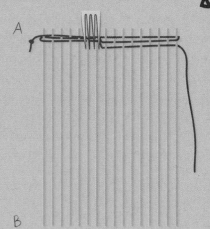

14. Hold the box vertically in front of you. The Celts worked with a standing loom, but in this case, you can hold the box however it's most comfortable. Place side A (with the knotted ends) on top. Starting at one of the top corners, run the needle over the first vertical string and under the second, over the third and under the fourth, and so on until you reach the end of a row. Pull gently until you reach the end of the yarn.

15. Start at the opposite side, going over the vertical threads you first went under, and under the vertical threads you first went over. Pull gently until you reach the end of the yarn. Go slowly—it's important you get the pattern right.

16. Continue for two or three rows, then use a fork to gently push up the yarn until you close any space between the horizontal rows.

17. Continue the same way until you fill about ¾ of the box.

18. Cut the remaining vertical threads by pairs and tie them together, keeping as close as possible to the cloth.

19. Open the knots in the strings on the opposite side so you can free the cloth from the box.

20. Tie the same strings again by pairs, keeping as close as possible to the cloth.

21. Cut the strings as short as you like, but be careful not to cut through the knots—they keep the cloth together.

Use the mat beneath a cup or a special object on your desk.

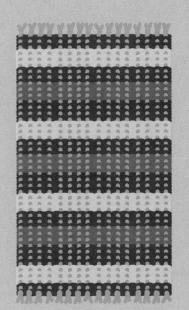

Celtic clothes were made of wool, which was spun into yarn, dyed different colors, and then woven into cloth using an upright loom. This task was usually performed by women, who created colorful patterns, mostly intersecting stripes. After the cloth was finished, they would cut and sew it to make clothes using a needle and yarn. Needles were initially made of bone. The oldest iron needles were found in Germany and date to the third century BC. Rich people wore tunics with strands of golden thread intertwined in the fabric.

Jewelry

All Celts, men and women, liked jewelry, especially necklaces, bracelets, and anklets. Almost everyone wore a special golden loop called a torque around the neck for good luck. Torques could be simple or have intricate designs.

Celtic torque, made in Gaul around the fourth or third century BC. Gift of J. Pierpont Morgan, 1917, to the Metropolitan Museum of Art, NY

Celtic jewels included precious stones and hardened resins like **amber** and **jet**, which were thought to have magical properties. When rubbed with wool, in fact, they discharge electricity, attracting hair and feathers. (The Greek word for amber was *electron*.) Large quantities of amber have been found in the Hallstatt graves.

ACTIVITY

Make a Celtic Torque

The two endings of torques could be as plain as small folds (to avoid sharp edges) and as elaborate as tiny sculptures. This activity teaches you how to make a torque with round endings.

Materials

2 pieces of heavy-duty aluminum foil, 2 inches square

2 sheets of 2-ply tissue paper, 4 inches square

Thin golden or silver headband

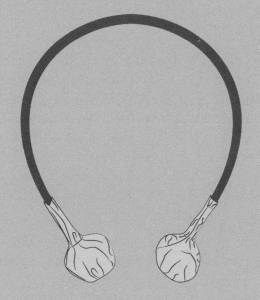

1. Place two pieces of aluminum foil on a clean surface.

2. Roll up two pieces of tissue paper until you form two small balls.

3. Place one ball in the center of each aluminum foil square.

4. Wrap each piece of foil around the ball. Leave the top portion (or stem) a little loose.

5. Stick one end of a headband through the stem of one of your balls. Press hard until the foil firmly grabs the headband and wrap the stem of the foil tightly around the headband.

6. Do the same at the other end of the headband.

7. Place it gently around your neck with the silver balls in front.

8. Wear it proudly like a Celtic warrior.

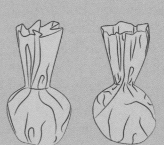

CELTIC WRITING

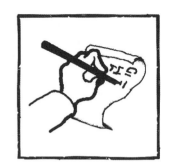

Like the Etruscans, the Celts left very few written documents. The largest texts were a calendar and a couple of legal documents, written around the first or second century BC. But this doesn't mean they didn't have literary talents.

Caecilius Statius, a Celt from a northern Italian tribe, became a celebrated poet after being sold as slave by the Romans in 222 BC. He composed 42 comic plays in Latin. Apparently, he never wrote a word in his mother tongue—or at least nothing survived.

Some believe that the Celtic religion forbade them from writing anything in their language. This would explain why Celtic literature flourished after Britain became Christian.

Today, ancient Celtic culture seems lost forever, though its original languages live on in modified forms. The two main Celtic languages have continued in Ireland, Wales, Western Scotland, Brittany, and the Isle of Man.

Many Celtic stories were recorded by Christian monks during the Middle Ages, though they made a few changes. They portrayed Celtic gods and goddesses in a negative light, sometimes demoting them to spirits and fairies. Some experts believe that the Irish leprechaun derived from the Celtic god Lugh, patron of the arts and of treasure, who was later called Lugh-Chromain ("little stooped Lugh").

King Arthur is a famous Celtic legend. The ninth-century monk Nennius claimed that his story was taken from a much earlier work. There are also references to this king in Welsh documents, leading experts to believe Arthur was an ancient Welsh king who was killed in battle.

Most of the surviving legends are from Ireland, which was left untouched by Rome. Many are included in cycles (sets) of stories. The Mythological Cycle, for example, talks of battles between supernatural races who invaded Ireland. The Ulster Cycle's main story is the Cattle Raid of Cooley, with about 80 related stories. The Ulster Cycle was constantly revised by storytellers who added slight modifications. The oldest version is based on two ninth-century manuscripts. The 11th-century version, *The Book of the Dun Cow*, is the most famous. Every version gives a general idea of the tales Celtic children might have been told while sitting around the fire.

THE ULSTER CYCLE

The Ulster Cycle starts when Queen Medb and her husband, Ailill, compared their individual riches to see who had more. They were even until the husband boasted about his white bull, an amazing creature with magical properties.

Filled with jealousy, Medb sent her messengers to find a comparable bull. Finally, she discovered there was one that was twice as valuable: the Brown Bull of Cooley. She sent her messengers to the owner, asking to borrow the bull for a year. The owner agreed, and everything would have been fine, but the messengers drank too much wine. They then revealed that the queen would have stolen the bull if the owner had said no. Offended, the owner took back his offer and a war started.

Two teenagers who had been friends, Cuchulain and Ferdiad, became leaders of opposing sides. In spite of Chuchulain's heroic fight, Medb managed to take the Brown Bull. The story ends with a fierce battle between the two bulls. The Brown Bull won but was mortally wounded. Before dying, he traveled the country, giving names to different places.

CELTIC ART AND MUSIC

Celtic art differed from place to place, but it usually had similar elements. Most of this art was used to decorate daily objects: helmets, shields, swords, mirrors, pots, furniture, jewelry, coins, and religious items.

The Celts' art was **stylized**, which means that when we look at an image, we recognize an object even if it doesn't look exactly like it. They preferred using symbols and outlines, even when they portrayed people. For example, the outline of a horse and a wheel on some Celtic coins represents a chariot.

The giant White Horse of Uffington is an interesting example of stylized Celtic art. It was created directly on a hill. The artist (or artists) dug trenches in the shape of a horse and filled them with crushed white chalk. This gigantic image was probably not meant only as artwork. It might have been devoted to the gods.

Stylized art focuses the viewer's attention on something other than the actual appearance of the object. In this case, attention is focused on the horse's energy, which is emphasized by its thin legs, which are detached from the body.

Celtic art often had geometric patterns—spirals, coils, circles, and swirling knots. Archaeological findings show that the Celts may have drawn their circles with a compass. Circles and swirls are used even in some portraits—circles for the eyes and swirls for the eyebrows and mustaches. This type of art has influenced modern art.

The White Horse of Uffington. Alan Denney, Flickr

Stone head of a Celtic man. It was found in a sacred place, so he might have been a warrior or a god. It is similar to other Celtic statues that were found across Europe. Eric Lessing / Art Resource, NY

Create a Stylized Celtic Picture

Both realistic and stylized images can be beautiful. The choice between the two can depend on the artist's taste or on the way the images will be used. Try your hand at both and discuss the results.

Materials

Paper

Pencil with eraser

Internet access (optional)

1. Fold a sheet of paper in half lengthwise.

2. On the left side, draw a picture of a person, animal, or thing. Try to be as realistic as possible.

3. On the right side of the paper, draw the same picture in a stylized manner. You may want to look at pictures of Celtic art online. To find the right time period, type "Celtic art iron age." You may also look at Celtic coins. Focus on drawing the strongest lines of the realistic image, those that most represent the shape or feeling of the object.

4. Once you are satisfied with your pictures, compare them to determine which one you like best and why. When do you think a stylized image would be best? On a logo? On a pattern? If you are doing this activity in a classroom, you and the other students can discuss your opinions.

Detail of a Celtic shield from Witham, Northern England. The large circle (which seems to have eyes) is held up by a fantastic creature with big eyes and strange ears. It might have frightened the enemy, suggesting that a strange creature was staring straight at his face. Erich Lessing / Art Resource, NY

Sometimes, the Celts hid stylized figures, especially human faces, inside geometric patterns. Many designs on Celtic objects had symbolic meanings that people at that time understood. Overall, the Celts portrayed more animals than humans. Their rare human portraits were usually limited to the head.

Celtic art has survived, with some variations, in Britain, especially in Christian crosses and books. A medieval copy of the Christian Gospel, known as the *Book of Kells,* is decorated with beautiful patterns that preserve the Celtic circles and swirls.

Music

Celtic instruments were probably similar to those used in nations around them, such as the lyre. The most original Celtic instrument was a war trumpet called a *carnyx.* The tube of the *carnyx* shot upward and ended with a wolf's head pointing outward instead of the usual trumpet bell. It sounded harsh and rough, like a loud croak. The *carnyx*'s sound and appearance frightened the enemy.

The official musicians (and poets) in Celtic society were called bards. They were well respected and even feared. Their songs could praise a man, improving his reputation, or put him to shame. Reputation was important in the ancient world. If someone had a bad reputation, it was not easy for him or her to move somewhere else. That's why powerful Celts made sure to invite bards to their feasts and paid them well to say good things about them.

Besides lifting or crushing the reputations of their hosts, bards sang popular stories that were passed from generation to generation. Since many of these stories included specific places and many characters, the bards also had to learn about the history and geography of their areas.

Today, Celtic music refers to traditional music of Ireland, Scotland, and Wales, as well as parts of France and Spain (Brittany and Galicia). No one knows when this traditional music started. The first mention of it is in a 12th-century book.

Make a Celtic Knot

Some medieval Celtic art includes decorations that look like long strings woven together to form interesting patterns. Today, these patterns are often known as Celtic knots. Try creating a simple Celtic knot with a piece of string. It's simpler than it sounds.

Materials

26-inch piece of string

Black marker

Red marker

Scrap paper

1. Place one end of the string on a piece of scrap paper and mark it with the black marker.

2. Place the other end of the string on the paper and mark it with the red marker. (This will help you with the directions.)

3. Take the string in your hand with the red end on your left and create a loop so that the black end of the string comes on top of the other.

4. Make a loop to the immediate right of the first one, going the opposite direction, so that the black end of the string comes on top of the other.

5. Insert the second loop into the first loop and pull slightly so that the black end of the string moves up. This will create a figure with three main holes.

6. Take the black end of your string and insert it through the bottom hole, coming from the back.

7. Now insert it through the second hole, going from front to back.

8. Insert it through the third hole, going from back to front.

9. Pull the string until your figure looks like a loose knot. You can arrange the knot to make it smaller or larger or change the shape slightly.

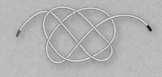

CELTIC RELIGION

The Celts apparently worshiped hundreds of gods, though many may have been the same gods with different names, depending on where they were worshiped. In fact, many aspects of Celtic religion varied from place to place.

Some Celtic Gods

Caesar wrote that Lugh, the most important god in Gaul, corresponded to the Roman Mercury. This must have seemed strange to the Romans, who considered Mercury a simple messenger of the gods. The Celtic Lugh was also a poet, musician, artist, craftsman, and physician and was often mentioned together with a goddess of wealth, Rosmerta. Archaeologists have confirmed Caesar's description, for there are statues of Lugh all over Gaul.

The second most important god, Caesar said, was Belenus, "the shining one," god of sun and fire and healing. He was the equivalent of the Roman Apollo. Other gods include Taranis, "the thunderer," equivalent of the Roman Jupiter; Cernunnos, a horned god associated with wild animals; and Epona, who protected horses. The Celts' god of war was worshiped with different names in various regions (and equivalent of the Roman Mars). So was the equivalent of the Roman Minerva, usually identified with the Celtic Brigid, goddess of healing, poetry, and fertility.

Each tribe or area had its own distinctive god or goddess. According to the Greek historian Timaeus, the favorite gods of the Celts who lived near the sea were twin brothers who suddenly appeared on the shore. Gods and goddesses were connected with natural elements, such as rivers, springs, trees, or stones. Water goddesses were particularly powerful.

The Gauls believed they descended from the same father, the god Dis (the Roman Pluto, god of the underworld). Since the underworld was a dark place, they counted their days beginning at sunset. If we did this today, Friday would begin on Thursday night.

Celts also gave great importance to birds, who lived between the world of men and the world of the gods. On the coast of Gaul, they kept on the lookout for two special crows, each with a white wing. When they spotted them, they would observe the way the birds ate to interpret it as a message from the gods.

Instead of building temples, the Celts worshiped in special woods that were considered sacred. They often carved images of their gods on tree trunks.

Druids and Vates

In Gaul and Britain, Celtic priests and priestesses were called druids. They were a special group of people who were carefully prepared for their religious tasks. Anyone could be a druid, but the training was difficult. Student druids had to work hard for 20 years to learn local laws and scientific notions, such as the motions of the stars and some natural events, as well as other subjects.

Many of the druids' rituals were secret and could not be written down, so the students had to memorize everything. To make it easier, they turned some texts into poetry, like today's children do with the ABC song. Once learned, they had to pass down the same knowledge to the next generation of druids.

Druids were greatly esteemed in their society. Their secret knowledge made them indispensable; if they were not around, no one knew the answers to certain questions. They also received special benefits: druids didn't have to pay taxes or fight wars.

Caesar met different druids during the eight years he spent in Gaul. One of them, Divitiacus, liked Caesar and was in favor of Roman rule. His brother, Dumnorix, opposed the Romans. Divitiacus spoke Latin well and had once visited Rome to ask for help against some Germanic tribes. There he had met the philosopher and politician Cicero and revealed to him Celtic techniques for predicting the future.

The druids' main religious task was to help people communicate with the gods and deliver divine messages back to the people. They also judged all sorts of cases—from small arguments to actual crimes. People liked to consult them before making major decisions. Druids could even stop an ongoing war if they thought the gods were against it. Their judgments were final. A different group of religious ministers, called vates, organized and performed animal sacrifices and interpreted any sign the gods might reveal.

Druids believed that murderers had to be killed; otherwise the nation could not prosper. If someone committed a terrible crime, druids could cut him off from the favor of the gods (and the people). This left criminals no choice but leave the tribe and wander off alone. In a dangerous world, it was the worst punishment that could be given.

Like other nations, the Celts sacrificed some condemned criminals to the gods, and the druids had to be present. This didn't happen very often.

Each tribe had a chief druid who held authority over the rest. When he died, he was succeeded by the most qualified druid. If there were contenders, the druids would vote. Sometimes, they raised armies and fought.

Eventually the Romans waged war on the Celtic druids. The main attack happened on the island of Anglesey, at the northwest tip of Wales, where druid rebels had assembled. Tacitus described the battle as frightening for the Roman soldiers, who were stunned by the strange sight of women dressed in black fighting in the army. With their wild hair and flaming torches, these women looked like the Furies, Greek goddesses of vengeance.

It took the Romans some time to regain their confidence. Finally, they attacked ferociously and won, killing the druids and destroying their altars and places of worship. The Romans claimed this utter destruction was due to the druids' practice of human sacrifice. In reality, the Romans were equally cruel in gladiatorial games. They were likely more concerned with the druids' great influence in the political life of the country, since these wise men were often hired as counselors to kings and tutors for children of noble families.

During World War II a building crew discovered over a hundred Celtic objects in a lake near Anglesey. There were weapons, shields, plaques, cauldrons, and pieces of chariots. Some think the Celts may have thrown these objects in the lake as an offering to the gods to receive their protection while the Romans approached.

In spite of the Romans' opposition, the druids continued their work. In Gaul, the Romans allowed them to build temples and worship. There are several accounts of Roman leaders meeting druids on peaceful terms and receiving advice from them.

There is an interesting story of a druidess who accused the Roman commander Diocletian of being stingy. He said that he would become generous as soon as he became emperor. She predicted he would reign, but only after killing a boar. Diocletian later had a chance to condemn a murderer named Aper, which meant "boar." He then remembered the prediction and killed Aper with his own hands. This man was a competitor to the throne, so by killing him Diocletian became emperor.

Diocletian's druidess ran a **tavern**, a place where people stopped to eat and drink. This seems to suggest that, in the third century BC, druids could not survive on donations alone and had to have other jobs.

OAKS, MISTLETOE, AND PLANT REMEDIES

Druids conducted some magical rituals, such as the collection of mistletoe. Celts believed that mistletoe had healing properties and could offset the effects of poison, even though mistletoe is very toxic in large quantities. They also believed it was a sacred plant, especially if it grew on oak trees. Because of this, only the druids could collect it, and they had to do it at night on the fifth day of the waxing moon, as the moon starts to grow.

On that special night, people prepared a banquet under the tree and brought two white bulls. Then the druids would come, dressed in white. Their chief would cut the mistletoe with a golden sickle. At that point, they would sacrifice the bulls to the gods, and then brew the mistletoe into a drink for animals who had stopped giving birth.

Besides the mistletoe, the druids normally picked and brewed other plants that were supposed to work as medicines or to increase the benefits of certain rituals. Pliny the Elder mentions three Celtic plants: glastum, selago, and samolus. Celtic women and young girls used glastum to stain their bodies to participate in rituals. Celts carried selago to prevent accidents. Samolus was supposed to be a remedy against sicknesses in pigs and cattle.

Celtic Feasts

The druids also led the Celts in celebrations. Archaeologists have found that the Celts had similar ways of organizing time, both in Britain and France. In each case, weeks lasted eight days. In Ireland, there were four seasons, with a festival at the start of each season. The main festival was called Samain. It marked the new year and was celebrated on the night that corresponds to our October 31. The Celts believed that this night was dangerous because the spirits of the dead roamed the Earth and anything could happen. Elements of these traditions survive in the United States and Europe as Halloween, in Latin America as Día de los Muertos, and in the Christian All Saints' Day.

The other festivals were Imbolc (February 1, to the Celtic goddess Brigid), Beltane (May 1, in honor of the god Belenus, marking when cattle were taken to higher pastures), and Lugnasad (August 1, a harvest festival dedicated to Lugh). In the first century BC, Lugnasad coincided with a general Council of Gauls.

CELTIC GOVERNMENT AND WARFARE

The main warriors in Celtic society were rulers who came from wealthy families with power and influence. They were usually men, but sometimes women led as well. Cartimandua, queen of the Brigantes, and Boudicca, queen of the Irenes, were two famous women rulers in the first century AD. Both were willing to ally with the Romans but were eventually disappointed. Cartimandua waited in vain for Roman troops to help her when she became dethroned, but Boudicca suffered the greatest wrong, being beaten, robbed, and abused. The Romans despised women rulers and thought the Celts were inferior for allowing women to rule.

Armor and Weapons

Greek writers say the Celts fought naked or half-naked, protected only by a helmet and shield. Judging by the sculptures and armor found in tombs, not everyone did that. Some believe the Romans learned to make chain mail armors from the Celts. It's understandable that naked warriors made the greatest impression on the enemy.

Celtic warriors wore bracelets and a torque for good luck. In 191 BC, when the Romans defeated the Celts in Bologna, Italy, they captured 1,500 gold torques.

Swords, spears, and slings were common weapons. Some used bows and arrows. Celtic swords were much larger than Roman swords. The historian Posidonius wrote they were as long as the spears of other nations. Short swords were more efficient in close combat, but the Celts swung their swords so skillfully they seldom allowed enemies to get close. Swords were great pieces of artwork. Handles were often forged in the shape of a warrior. Some had two corals placed just below the handle, like dragon eyes. Because swords were expensive, some warriors only had a dagger and a sling, which could do a lot of harm.

Spears were more affordable than swords. They were made of wood with a small metal piece at the end. Celtic spears were also longer than Roman spears, and had large iron heads, often shaped in a spiral to tear through the enemies' flesh as it entered and was pulled back. They could do a lot of damage when thrown from a distance, but then they could be lost.

Shields were rectangular or oval and almost as large as a person. They were usually made from one piece of wood covered with leather, with metal decorations that were also used to hit the enemy during a fight.

Celtic helmets could be very scary. They were usually made of bronze with frightening images on top—horns, birds, or boars—that made the soldiers look even taller. Archaeologists have found a Celtic helmet topped by a large raven with flapping wings. Celts believed the gods took the form of a raven from time to time, often when they

Make a Celtic Sword

The Celts were very proud of their swords and often enriched them with precious stones and symbolic images. Some placed the stones so they looked like eyes. Make a cardboard sword and decorate it as you like.

Materials

Cardboard box (strong, but easy to cut)

Pencil

Scissors

Silver duct tape

Gold duct tape (optional)

Golden acrylic paint

Paintbrush

Black marker

Glue

Small acrylic jewels (or buttons)

1. With the pencil, draw a sword on a piece of cardboard.

2. Cut it out with scissors.

3. Cover both sides of the blade portion with silver duct tape. This will make the blade stronger and make it look like metal.

4. Use gold paint or gold duct tape to color the grip of the sword.

5. Use gold paint to color both sides of the sword's cross guard (between the grip and blade).

6. Place the sword upright against a support so that the cross guard can dry without touching any surface.

7. Once the cross guard is dry, use the marker to draw any Celtic-inspired design you like.

8. Glue acrylic jewels to the cross guard.

escorted a dead person to the afterlife. A raven on a helmet suggested death to the enemy. Some Celts even placed horned helmets on their horses' heads.

Attaching objects to a helmet was not always wise, because an enemy could easily grab them to throw the helmet on the ground. This choice of helmets and the fact that some warriors fought naked suggest that the Celts were more interested in frightening the enemy than in protecting themselves.

Celtic chariots astonished foreign enemies. They were simple platforms on two iron wheels with wooden spokes, and seated only two men: a driver and a warrior. These men's skills amazed Julius Caesar, especially their ability "to gallop their teams down the steepest of slopes without loss of control."

CHICKEN LITTLES?

As terrifying as the Celts appeared in battle, there was a rumor they had a secret fear: they were afraid that the sky would fall on their heads. How did the rumor start?

According to a Greek story, in 335 BC the powerful ruler Alexander the Great arranged a meeting with the representatives of some Celtic tribes. During the meeting, he asked them what they feared the most. Their reply surprised him: "We fear nothing, except that the sky might fall on our heads."

Alexander thought the Celts were arrogant. They probably meant that they feared only the gods. In any case, the story was told and retold until some people actually believed the Celts were scared that the sky might fall, like the story of Chicken Little.

Chariots could appear almost out of nowhere with incredible noise as the iron wheels hit stones along the way. While the drivers controlled the chariots, the warriors hurled javelins at their enemies. Some warriors were so skillful that they could throw spears while balancing on the pole connecting the chariot to the horses. When they reached the main battle, the warriors would grab their swords, jump off the chariots, and fight in close combat. The drivers would turn the horses in a flash, move to safety, and return to pick up the warriors in trouble. It all happened with incredible mastery and speed.

The Romans admired the Celts' horsemanship and recruited many into their cavalry. Historians believe the Romans learned to ride horses from the Celts. Occasionally they used Celtic-style saddles, which had four knobs—two in front and two in back. The knobs kept the riders on the horses by holding their hips in place. On these saddles, riders could stretch their torsos to the left and the right without falling.

Military Strategy

When battling each other, Celtic tribes chose one man to fight from each tribe. This was a better way to settle arguments because fewer people died. With few exceptions, when Celts came into contact with Roman and Greek armies, they changed their tactic to all-out warfare.

Before a battle, the Celts made lots of noise by shouting, stomping, blowing trumpets, and banging their swords on their shields. Caesar said that the Celts in Britain painted their bodies blue with dye extracted from the leaves of the **woad** plant. Woad was normally used to dye cloth, and it's not effective in coloring skin. It's possible the Celts used it to mark their bodies before battle but, since the plant was well known for its healing properties, it's also possible they used it after a battle to treat their wounds.

Apparently, after battle the Celts hung the heads of their enemies from their horses' necks, brought them home, and nailed them to the entrance of their homes. If the heads belonged to famous warriors, the Celts would preserve them with cedar oil, then post them at the city walls to threaten outsiders. Some skulls were posted in temples, and some victims were sacrificed as burned offerings to the Celtic gods.

This was not just a Celtic tradition. Other populations throughout the world did the same. The Greeks and Romans, however, considered the custom barbaric.

According to Roman authors, despite their frightening behavior, the Celts had serious military weakness because they didn't follow a strategy. They preferred to gather in large numbers instead of dividing their forces into strategic locations. This impulsiveness helped their enemies, who could provoke them to behave the same way each time.

Another weakness was their disunity. Like the Etruscans, the Celts were not united as one people and often fought each other.

The woad plant in bloom. Pethan, Wikimedia Commons

CELTIC DAILY LIFE

Since the Celts lived across Europe, they didn't all live exactly the same way, though they had many things in common. According to Caesar, the only two classes of any importance in Celtic society were the druids and the warriors. The rest, in his opinion, were not much better than slaves. It was an exaggeration, but it shows that there was a large gap between the ruling class and the common people.

Occupations and Products

Most Celts were farmers or shepherds. Some were artisans or merchants. Those who lived near natural deposits of minerals such as copper, iron, and salt built mines and spent their lives digging for these treasures. Salt made the people of Hallstatt rich. The skeletons found in those graves show that even the wealthy worked hard all their lives. Specifically, the skeletons of men showed signs of heavy workload on both shoulders, and those of women only on one, leading historians to think that men did the digging while women carried the salt out of the mines over one shoulder. According to archaeologists, the Celts at Hallstatt dug over 650 miles of tunnels.

The Celts were skilled metalworkers, and their products were famous all over Europe. Working metal was hard work. To make a sword, a blacksmith had to heat up a long piece of metal until it was red hot, then beat it repeatedly with a hammer. When it started to cool down, he had to place it back into hot coals, continually repeating the process until he produced a flat, sharp sword.

Iron is a difficult metal to shape, but the Celts were able to bend it so perfectly as to cover a wooden wheel or to bind a wooden barrel. The metal had to be applied to the wheel or the barrel when it was still hot, holding the wood in place after it cooled down. Some historians believe the Celts invented the barrel. They also created an impressive threshing machine with sharp teeth that could harvest corn while being pushed forward by an ox.

Celtic products varied from region to region. The most common were wheat, millet, rye, barley, beans, peas, and lentils. Farmers raised sheep for their wool, goats and cows for their milk, chicken for eggs and meat, oxen for pulling plows and wagons, horses for transportation and warfare, and dogs for hunting. The Celts in northern Italy learned from the Etruscans how to grow grapes and produce wine, and took acorns from the natural oak forests to raise pigs.

Slavery was common throughout the ancient world. For the Celts, slaves were a main export, along with metals, salt, and hunting dogs. A slave chain found in northern Wales has five sets of neck shackles and was probably used to transport groups of slaves from one place to another. These shackles were painful and uncomfortable, forcing the slaves to keep their heads low and still. The Romans imported slaves from Britain, often in exchange for gallons of wine.

When noblemen were not fighting, they managed their business by overseeing their properties and trading goods. In their free time, they hunted, fished, and played with friends. They also had horse races, usually during festivals.

Women and Children

According to Greeks and Romans, Celtic women were as tall and strong as their men. They also had more legal rights than Greek and Roman women and could own personal property. But husbands were still the head of the home and had power of life and death over their families. When a woman married, she left her tribe to join the tribe of her husband.

In most families, Celtic children learned to work around the house at a young age. Only the sons of noblemen, or those who trained as druids, received a higher education. In any case, they probably found time to play with simple toys. Archaeologists have found colorful glass beads with Celtic designs that may have been used as marbles.

According to Julius Caesar, Celtic boys could only be seen in public with their fathers after they were of fighting age. Even then, they were often sent to live with families in other tribes, probably to strengthen ties between tribes. This system was called fostering. Sometimes the children became more loyal to their new tribe than to their own. If a war broke out between the two tribes, the new tribe could hold the foster children hostage.

In some cases, tribal leaders gave people from their tribe (including their family members) as voluntary hostages to another tribal leader after making a deal. Even Caesar took advantage of this system. Unsure if a Celtic leader would keep his word, Caesar asked him to give him 200 hostages, including his son and some relatives. After the conditions of the treaty were met, the hostages could return home.

CELTIC FOOD

Feasts were important occasions for Celts and often marked special events. People sat on the grass around low wooden tables, where bread and a great quantity of meat were served. The meat was either stewed in a cauldron with herbs and vegetables or cooked on skewers over an open fire.

Everyone waited for the guest of honor, who sat at the head of the table, to take the first portion. This person could be the chief of the tribe, the most valiant warrior, or a wealthy man. Next to him was the host of the feast. The other guests sat according to their importance or rank: the most important next to these two men, and the less important farther away. After the main guest took his portion, the others started to take chunks of meat with their hands or cut off a piece at a time with a small knife.

A Greek author named Phylarchus wrote about a huge feast given by a rich Celt named Ariamnes. Ariamnes was not satisfied giving a simple dinner party. He announced he would give his countrymen a banquet every year.

His plan was ingenious. He divided the land into sections, then he marked the limits of each section by placing tents made with poles, straw, and branches along the road. These tents were large enough to host 400 men or more. Inside the tents "he placed huge cauldrons, full of every sort of meat," including beef, pork, and lamb. He also prepared an abundance of wine and bread. Finally, he invited not only the local Celts, but even strangers who passed by.

Ariamnes might have been especially generous, or he might have been trying to gain popularity so he could be chosen as a leader. In any case, inviting foreigners to banquets was quite common among Celts. According to Diodorus, they didn't even ask people who they were until after the banquet was over. Sadly, some Roman commanders took advantage of this practice to enter Celtic villages and kill all the people.

The best feasts included lots of beer and wine, which—unlike Greeks and Romans—the Celts drank undiluted. In the tomb of a Gallic princess, archaeologists have found a wine-mixing bowl that could hold 260 gallons of wine. Another tomb included a drinking horn that could hold about 1½ gallons. The Celts who lived in north Italy or Turkey learned to make excellent wine.

Beer was made from wheat or barley. The Celts of ancient Britain, France, Spain, and Germany were all skilled brewers. The Greeks and Romans thought beer was an uncultured drink. The Roman emperor Julian, who ruled between AD 360 and 363, tasted beer during a visit to Germany and thought it smelled like goats.

Corma, a strong drink made by fermenting large quantities of summer honey mixed with water, was the most affordable alcoholic beverage among Celts. *Corma* was often served at meals in communal cups or drinking horns that were passed from left to right. (Handing it from right to left would have been an offense to the gods.) In a Celtic tomb near Hochdorf, Germany, archaeologists have found a large cauldron, decorated with three lions around the brim, which was once filled with *corma*.

But Celtic feasts were not always peaceful. They were occasions where a man could show off his status and wealth, and if someone felt robbed of the honor he thought he deserved, he could challenge his rival to a duel.

Everyday Celtic meals were more modest, with an abundance of grains and beans. If hunting was good, the Celts ate venison. In the cold climate of northern Europe, soups were plentiful.

They also made butter and stored it underground in **bogs** (muddy areas), inside barrels, pots, or animal skins. Quite recently an Irish man found a 2,000-year-old, 22-pound lump of butter in one of those bogs. This is not the first discovery of this kind. Once in a while, people find barrels of either butter or animal fat stored underground. The cool environment of a northern bog serves as a natural refrigerator.

Make Butter

Pliny called butter "the most delicate of food" among the people Greeks called barbaric. He thought it had medicinal properties too. To make butter, he said, these people poured milk in a tall vase and shook it. You can use a similar method to make your own batch of butter.

Materials

Measuring cup

¼ cup of heavy cream

Jar with lid, large enough to hold one cup or more of liquid

Small mesh strainer

Bowl

Piece of plastic wrap, about 4 inches long

1. Measure the cream, then pour it into a jar.

2. Close the jar tightly and shake it energetically. This process will take some time, so if you have a friend who can help you, you can take turns.

3. At first, you will see the cream fill the whole jar. If you stopped now, this would be whipped cream. Keep shaking. You will eventually hear the sound of liquid splashing again inside the jar. Shake a little longer, for a total of 15 to 20 minutes.

4. Place a strainer over a bowl, open the jar, and pour the contents into the strainer. The lump you see is butter.

5. Place a piece of plastic wrap on a table and put the butter in the middle.

6. Wrap the plastic around the butter and refrigerate. When it's solid, you can either use it right away or wait for a special occasion. As for the liquid in the bowl, you can use it in cooking. Mix it into pancake batter—then spread the pancakes with your fresh butter.

PART IV: THE CARTHAGINIANS

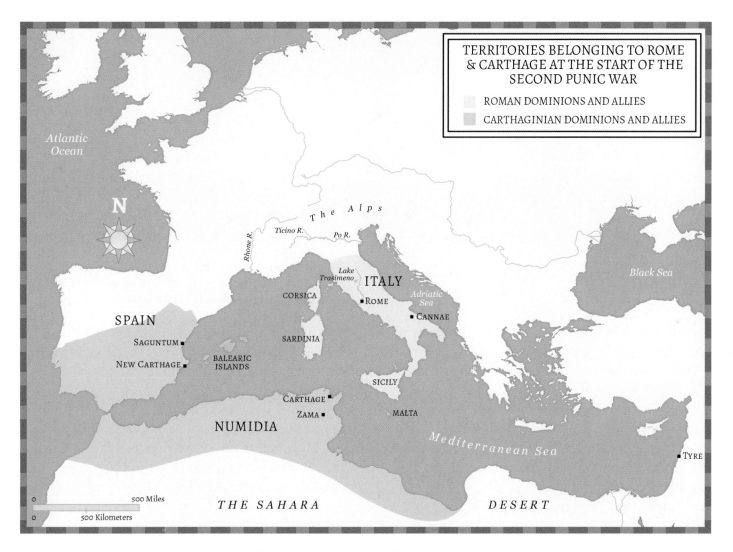

TERRITORIES BELONGING TO ROME & CARTHAGE AT THE START OF THE SECOND PUNIC WAR

ROMAN DOMINIONS AND ALLIES

CARTHAGINIAN DOMINIONS AND ALLIES

Atlantic Ocean

N

The Alps

Rhone R.

Ticino R.

Po R.

Lake Trasimeno

ITALY

CORSICA

ROME

Adriatic Sea

CANNAE

SPAIN

SAGUNTUM

SARDINIA

NEW CARTHAGE

BALEARIC ISLANDS

Black Sea

SICILY

CARTHAGE

ZAMA

MALTA

NUMIDIA

Mediterranean Sea

TYRE

500 Miles

500 Kilometers

THE SAHARA

DESERT

The Cathaginians in the Mediterranean

CARTHAGINIAN HISTORY

Carthage was originally a colony of Phoenicia, a prosperous civilization in the area that is now Lebanon. The Phoenicians built many colonies around the Mediterranean Sea as rest stops for their frequent travels. Carthage was founded around the eighth century BC.

The Greeks and Romans told an unusual story about the founding of Carthage. They said a beautiful princess fled Tyre, an ancient Phoenician city, after her brother murdered her husband. She traveled west by boat, looking for a place to build a new city and start a new life. When she arrived in the area where Carthage stands today, she asked the local ruler for just enough land as could be enclosed by the skin of an ox. Probably thinking that she would pitch a tent, the ruler gave her permission. Instead, she cut an ox hide into many thin strips and laid them one after another, tip to tip, around a hill. She called it Qart Hadasht, which meant "new city" in Phoenician. The hill was called Byrsa, which meant "fortress" in Phoenician and "ox hide" in Greek.

In the earliest version of the story, her countrymen tried to force her to marry a man from Lebanon. She disliked the idea so much she killed herself by jumping into a burning pyre.

Years later, the Roman poet Virgil gave the story another twist. He said that the Trojan hero Aeneas, in his journey from Troy (in today's Turkey) to the area where Rome was to be founded, stopped at Carthage and met this beautiful princess. She fell in love with him.

He stayed with her for a while, but in the end, he told her he had to continue his journey. It was his destiny, he said. The princess was so heartbroken she killed herself by jumping into a burning pyre.

Before dying she cursed Rome, vowing that Carthage would make it pay for what Aeneas had done to her. To the Romans, this was why Rome and Carthage were such fierce enemies. In the earliest story, she was named Elissa; in Virgil's story her name was Dido.

Carthage in the Mediterranean

The Carthaginians relied on Phoenicia only until the eighth century BC, when the Assyrians took over the region. After that, the Carthaginians took responsibility of protecting and regaining Phoenician territories in the west while establishing new colonies. By the end of the sixth century, they had gained control of much of North Africa as well as the islands of Corsica, Sardinia, Malta, the Balearics, and part of Sicily. Any ship sailing the Mediterranean had to pass Carthaginian lands.

For centuries Greece was Carthage's strongest enemy. In 323 BC, Alexander the Great, who had already occupied Phoenicia, raised a fleet to invade Carthage, Italy, and Spain. Fortunately for Carthage, he died before he could launch his plan.

The Carthaginians were so good at trading that by the third century BC Carthage was the richest nation in the Mediterranean. Its territories were larger and more profitable than the Romans'. It had a large population, about 300,000 people, as people were drawn to the prosperous city.

This influence and strength made Carthage a serious threat for Rome, which was not about to remain idle, especially since Carthage owned part of Sicily, an island located between the two capitals. Sicily was a great producer of wheat, which was a main part of the Mediterranean diet.

The fight for Sicily, which lasted from 264 to 241 BC, is known as the First Punic War. Romans used the adjective *punicus* to refer to the Carthaginians. Initially, Carthage had the upper hand thanks to its huge ships, called **quinqueremes**, each of which carried about 300 men. These ships were fast, strong, powerful, and easy to steer, all at the same time. With as many as 350 quinqueremes, Carthage had the largest fleet in the Mediterranean.

The Romans discovered an abandoned Carthaginian ship and studied it to see how it was made. By copying every detail, they were able to make their own quinqueremes, and the battle continued. The first Roman quinqueremes were not as good as those from Carthage. The Romans used green wood, so the ships didn't last more than a year.

But that's all the time the Romans needed to turn things around. The Carthaginian ships were often weighed down with grain and supplies while the Romans, being closer to home, didn't need as much cargo. Eventually the Carthaginian general, Hamilcar Barca, was forced to surrender. The defeat was especially humiliating because it happened at sea, where the Carthaginians were champions.

The Romans took about 30,000 Carthaginian prisoners and demanded a large sum of money from Carthage each year, called tribute. Losers in war had to submit to whatever terms the winners chose.

Hannibal, as portrayed by a Roman artist. Alinari / Art Resource, NY

In spite of its riches, which allowed Carthage to pay the fee sooner than the Romans expected, the loss came at a difficult time. Carthage was dealing with a violent rebellion of **mercenary** soldiers it had hired from other countries. The soldiers were angry because they were not paid what Carthage had promised.

The rebellion turned into a war that lasted over three years and spread to other Carthaginian territories, including Sardinia. The threat was so serious that the Carthaginians, already heavily taxed, put all their jewels into a common fund to finance the war. Carthage eventually squelched the rebellion and worked hard, once again, to rebuild its riches.

In 237 BC, Hamilcar moved to Spain with the intention of founding a new Carthaginian colony. Spain was rich in silver—a precious metal Carthage needed to get back on its feet. He also nurtured a more urgent plan: train a new army to attack Rome.

In Spain, he continued to conquer territory until 228 BC, when he died in battle. His second-in-command, Hasdrubal "the Fair," took over the army. Hasdrubal continued the conquest and built a new city in Spain, called New Carthage (today's Cartagena). When Hasdrubal was killed in 221 BC, Hamilcar's firstborn son, Hannibal, took his place.

Beating the Odds

Hannibal had traveled with the Carthaginian army since he was nine. He begged his father to take him along to Spain, and Hamilcar agreed on one condition: Hannibal had to have a life-long hatred of Rome and vow to bring down the Roman empire.

Now Hannibal was 25 and eager to fulfil his vow. The troops knew him well and supported his leadership. He became the most formidable enemy the republic of Rome ever faced.

Well aware of Hannibal's goal, the Roman Senate made an alliance with the Spanish city of Saguntum. It was an interference Hannibal could not allow. When Hannibal destroyed Saguntum, Rome knew that war was inevitable.

The Roman Senate assigned military operations to Publius Cornelius Scipio, a trusted general, who prepared his troops for Spain. Scipio was confident he could crush the young Carthaginian because his army was much larger than Hannibal's.

But Hannibal had a different plan. He didn't want to fight in Spain. He wanted to attack Rome. Since the Romans controlled lands on the Mediterranean, Hannibal decided to attack Rome from an unexpected direction, the north. In the spring of 218 BC, he set out on what seemed an impossible mission: he marched by land across Spain, then across the Alps, the highest chain of mountains in Europe.

The march was even more impractical because Hannibal took along 37 North African elephants. Carthage had used elephants in battle for many years. They were used much like today's tanks. They had to be trained; otherwise they could panic and turn against their handlers. According to some experts, North African elephants were smaller than their Indian and African cousins.

On his march, Hannibal had to deal with the Celtic tribes along the way. Some were peaceful and even helped him in exchange for rewards. Others attacked him, seeing him as an intruder to be robbed or expelled. These skirmishes were tough because the local tribes knew the territory much better, but they served as training for Hannibal's army.

France's Rhône River was his first major obstacle. A large tribe of pro-Roman Celts had gathered on the opposite side where they expected Hannibal to cross. Hannibal tricked them by instructing an officer to lead a group of soldiers across the river at a different point.

Immediately after crossing, the officer built a signal fire for Hannibal, who started to cross the river toward the enemy's camp. Just before the Celts struck, the other Carthaginian soldiers attacked them from behind, forcing them to flee.

Hannibal's men built large log rafts to transport his elephants across the river. Since elephants are easily frightened, they covered the rafts with soil and grass to make the animals believe they were on solid ground.

By October, Hannibal and his men reached the Alps. They were tired, having traveled more than 600 miles. It was also the worst time of the year to cross the mountain chain. The approaching winter could bring snowstorms and avalanches. Waiting for spring was risky, too, because Rome would have time to hear about Hannibal's approach.

On the way up the mountains, Hannibal began to suffer great losses. Some elephants fell into ravines and died. Frostbite was common, and many men froze to death. Rations were short and morale was low. Because Hannibal had no maps, sometimes the soldiers had to retrace their steps.

The army also found giant rocks blocking the trail. The only way to proceed was to cut a pathway through the rock, which seemed impossible. But Hannibal was prepared even for this. He had taken along large quantities of vinegar. Ancient scientists had discovered that vinegar and heat combined together to erode the lime found in many rocks. Hannibal's men hit the rocks to create large gaps, then cut trees and leaned them against the rocks. When the wind was favorable, they set fire to the trees and waited until the rocks were scalding hot. They then poured boiling vinegar into the gaps. The vinegar weakened the rocks, allowing the men to break them apart with iron tools.

Hannibal Against Rome

Hannibal descended down the Alps through Italy on his way to face the Roman army. He had left New Carthage with 46,000 men and

Elephant on the back of a Carthaginian coin. Classical Numismatic Group

had arrived with 26,000, all exhausted and starving. They were, however, the strongest and fittest soldiers. Soon they found food in the northern villages, and fresh courage.

The Roman guards who first saw the Carthaginians must have been shocked: elephants descending from the Alps? News soon reached Rome, and Scipio led a Roman cavalry to the Ticino River, near the Alps. Once again, Scipio was confident. Defeating a small and weary Carthaginian army didn't seem difficult.

The Carthaginians, however, had trained for this moment for years. They knew Romans attacked their enemies head-on, so they moved rapidly around them, attacking them by surprise. Scipio was gravely wounded and quickly defeated. The Carthaginians used the same tactics to defeat the Romans at Lake Trasimeno, about 100 miles north of Rome, and then again near the city of Cannae, on the Adriatic Sea.

The Romans didn't understand Hannibal's strategy. They kept counting on their numbers. The Roman Senate sent the largest army in its history, 86,000 men, to Cannae. By that time, Hannibal had 50,000 men, largely Celts from northern Italy who had joined his forces. Unlike the Roman generals, Hannibal led the way, together with the Celts, while the cavalry followed. Behind the cavalry was his original group of veteran Carthaginians.

Confident, the Roman army moved against Hannibal. Their excitement rose when they saw the Carthaginians gradually retreating. They didn't know that Hannibal had instructed his veterans to pretend to retreat in order to move slowly to the sides. The huge Roman army soon found itself surrounded by Carthaginians, with hardly any room to move around. Hannibal's cavalry pushed the Roman cavalry back. He then ordered his veterans to attack the Romans from every side. It all happened so suddenly that some Romans didn't even understand what was happening.

In the bloodshed that followed, about 70,000 Romans died and 10,000 were taken prisoner. Scipio escaped. It was the greatest defeat in Roman history. Walking through the sea of corpses, Hannibal took the rings off the hands of patricians and sent them to Carthage as proof of his victory.

Hannibal's Loss

At that point, everyone in Rome expected Hannibal to attack them. Having lost 80,000 men, the citizens would be forced to surrender. But he didn't. Historians have wondered why. Most likely he didn't have enough men and weapons, such as catapults and battering rams, to sustain a siege of the city. Instead, he sent his brother Mago to Carthage with the rings and requested help. In the meantime, he sent a messenger to the Roman Senate to negotiate a surrender.

The Roman Senate refused to give up and sent the messenger away. If Rome had shown itself to be weak, that would have been its end. Mago's mission to Carthage was also unsuccessful. Afraid of what might happen if Hannibal lost, the Carthaginian Senate refused to help. Left to himself, Hannibal continued to raid Italian towns, hoping that Rome would react and fight him in the field again, but this time Rome didn't take the bait.

In the meantime, a new Publius Cornelius Scipio (son of the other general) gathered a new army. After such a loss of able soldiers, he had to change some rules: he recruited younger men, slaves, and prisoners by promising them freedom. Rome doubled its taxes to finance the war, but few complained. It was their last chance.

Scipio had a plan. Instead of facing Hannibal on the field in Italy, where Rome would likely lose, he attacked Spain and conquered Carthage's territories. He then sailed to Carthage, forcing Hannibal to return.

Hannibal could have refused to help Carthage, since its senate never helped him. Instead, he returned in 202 BC, for the first time since he was nine. In a battlefield near the ancient city of Zama, Hannibal discovered the Romans had learned their lesson. Scipio copied Hannibal's tactics and defeated him—for the first time in Hannibal's life. It was the end of the second cycle of battles between Rome and Carthage, known as the Second Punic War. Later, the Roman Senate voted to award Scipio the name Africanus as a testimony of his victory at Zama.

Zama marked the beginning of the end for Carthage. Soon all of North Africa was conquered by Rome. The Carthaginian Senate was forced to accept Scipio's terms. Blaming Hannibal for the defeat, they decided to deliver him to the Romans.

Warned of the plot, Hannibal left Carthage and Africa, never to return. Instead, he offered his services to anyone who shared his hatred for Rome. The Romans hunted Hannibal down to make him pay for the destruction he had caused. When they finally found him at the court of the king of Bithynia (in today's Turkey), he took poison to avoid capture. He was 63.

Carthage Must Be Destroyed

Once again, Rome demanded large sums of money from Carthage. It also dictated that Carthage could never mobilize an army again. The second command was difficult to keep because the neighboring nation of Numidia, who had allied with Rome, kept invading Carthaginian territory. The Carthaginians tried to obey the rules and asked Rome for help, but when Rome failed to respond, they broke their agreement and fought Numidia. Once again, Rome asked them to pay a huge fine. In spite of these setbacks, Carthage had enough resources to restore its impressive harbor.

Some Roman leaders were concerned. A nation so quick to bounce back was a serious threat, especially one so close to Rome. One of these senators, Cato the Elder, was so convinced of this threat that he ended all of his speeches saying, "Carthage must be destroyed." Once, to give strength to his words, he hid figs in the fold of his toga and let them fall to the ground during his speech. When other senators admired the freshness and beauty of the fruits, he explained that they came from Carthage, only three days away. In other words, "This is how long it would take for a Carthaginian army to land in Italy."

Not every senator agreed with Cato. Publius Cornelius Scipio Nasica, cousin of Scipio Africanus, returned from a mission to Carthage with the opposite conclusion: keeping Carthage as a threat and competitor would help Rome to stay humble and on guard. But Cato convinced the Senate to attack. In 149 BC, Rome sent troops against Carthage, starting the Third Punic War.

Over the centuries, Romans have reflected on the discussion between Cato and Scipio Nasica and concluded that Scipio was right. As Rome became freer from external threats, it became more careless and corrupt.

Heroic Resistance

In spite of their disadvantage, the Carthaginians resisted. The Romans had deprived them of ships and weapons, so they built new ones. Everyone—men, women, and children—went to work. They used every resource, including metal objects and materials they had used to strengthen their homes. Women cut off their hair to make rope for the catapults, and slaves were set free to fight willingly.

According to historians, every day the Carthaginians produced 140 shields, 300 swords, 500 spears and javelins, and many bolts and catapults. Because of their commitment, the siege continued for two years, longer than the Romans expected. In the end, the Romans sent a new commander, Scipio Aemilianus, the adopted grandson of Scipio Africanus.

Scipio focused on cutting off supplies to Carthage. The city had been able to receive supplies by sea, so Scipio built a long line of fortifications around the city, including a large stone wall across the mouth of the harbor, and set his ships as guards. Not a bite of food could enter the city.

The starving Carthaginians resisted to the end. When Scipio and his men scaled the city walls and entered the city, he found people still ready to fight. Finally, he set fire to the city.

The Greek historian Polybius, who was an eyewitness of these events, saw Scipio crying at the sight of the burning Carthaginian capital. Scipio quoted a line from Homer's famous poem *The Iliad*: "A day will come when sacred Troy shall perish." When Polybius asked him what he meant, he said he feared the day when Rome would meet the same end. If the great and powerful Carthage could be utterly destroyed, so could Rome.

The burning of Carthage was unusual because the Romans rarely destroyed cities. They preferred to keep them and their riches as their own property. In this case, however, only the harbor survived to be used for commercial ships. They rebuilt the city a century later, but with a different, Roman look.

The Carthaginians After Carthage

The Romans named the new city Julia Carthago and made it the capital of the province. The new city grew and prospered, and by the early second century AD it was the third-largest city in the Roman Empire. It also became an active center of Christianity, giving birth to authors, such as Cyprian and Tertullian, and famous martyrs, such as Perpetua and Felicita.

Carthage was destroyed again in AD 698 by Islamic troops and rebuilt as Tunis, which is today the capital of Tunisia. Some ruins of Carthage are still visible on the outskirts of Tunis.

In the meantime, many Carthaginians who had emigrated to other parts of the world continued to spread their culture. The Carthaginian model of government was adopted in many North African countries, and the Punic language carried on for centuries, both in rural areas around Carthage and in other nations.

CARTHAGINIAN ARCHITECTURE

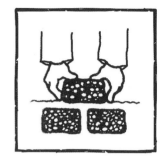

The Carthaginians were rich enough to build an impressive city with two gigantic harbors, beautiful temples, and comfortable homes. They were also close to natural deposits of limestone, which was easy to mine and work. Archaeologists believe the Carthaginians adopted a quarrying method that was already familiar to the Egyptians. They marked the edge of a stone block with a chisel, stuck a piece of wood into the crack, and wet the wood. The water caused the wood to swell, making the crack wider.

Even though the Romans burned Carthage to the ground, archaeologists have found enough written descriptions, sculptures, and ruins (both in Carthage and nearby) to have a general idea of its appearance.

The city was built on a thin strip of land with the Mediterranean Sea on both sides, and was defended from the mainland by a series of 23-mile-long walls. It was an ideal location to control incoming and outgoing ships. Carthage was likely the largest city in the ancient world after Alexandria, and equally lavish.

The Harbors

Carthage's harbors were an architectural marvel. By the second century, they were superior to any others in the Mediterranean Sea. Naturally just one big harbor, it was then divided in half, one half for trade and one for war, with a single entrance from the sea. This entrance was about 70 feet wide (about two city busses parked end to end) and closed by chains.

The entrance gave way to the rectangular commercial harbor, with docks on either side. Just behind that was the military harbor, with a tall, round building in the middle for the admiral. Thirty docks surrounded the building, and 140 more along the wider circle. This served two purposes: ships could move quickly out of the

Painting showing reproduction of Carthage's military harbor. Erich Lessing / Art Resource, NY

TEMPLES AND TOMBS

Like many ancient cities, Carthage had temples dedicated to its gods and goddesses. The most spectacular was the temple of Eshmun, the Phoenician god of healing, which stood atop a hill reached by climbing 60 steps.

All the original temples are now destroyed, but some stone carvings give a general idea of their appearance. Like temples in Egypt and Phoenicia, they had flat roofs, front porches lined with columns, and inner rooms for the worship of the god or goddess. Their outsides were decorated with geometric patterns or symbolic images. Inside, there were images of the gods and altars where priests could offer sacrifices.

There were likely other religious buildings. For example, in the ancient Tunisian city of Dougga there is a **mausoleum** (tomb) with an inscription in both Punic (the Carthaginian language) and Libyan. This three-level building is 70 feet high—as tall as the White House. It's topped by a pyramid and decorated with ornamental columns and reliefs. This mausoleum is different from other Greek and Roman buildings but was popular around Carthage. It looked like lighthouses that were common at that time.

The mausoleum at Dougga. Institute for the Study of the Ancient World, Wikimedia and Flickr

harbor, and the admiral could spot approaching ships, which could not see inside the harbor.

A series of walls separated the harbors from the city. Besides being practical, they were also beautiful, dazzling visitors with impressive marble columns—two for each dock.

The main town square was next to the harbor, where merchants sold their goods and the citizens met for special functions and announcements.

Homes

At its peak, Carthage was a beautiful city with comfortable homes and delightful gardens. One of its districts, called Megara, was particularly luxurious, "planted with gardens and . . . full of fruit-bearing trees divided off by low walls, hedges, and brambles, besides deep ditches full of water running in every direction."

Carthage's richest and largest homes were built on the slopes of hills, where they were better protected from raiders. Their walls were covered with plaster, which shined in the sun like marble. The city was much more beautiful and comfortable than Rome, which, at that time, was still a small, crowded town.

Many Carthaginian homes were similar to the Roman *domus* and included central courtyards surrounded by rooms—often with built-in cupboards, chests, and bread ovens. Some had second floors with balconies. Like many Mediterranean homes today, they had flat roofs reached by a flight of stairs. These rooftops were like terraces where people could enjoy the sunshine in cooler months, or cool off on summer nights. They usually had a high wall to protect people from falling off.

In the ruins of a city near Carthage, archaeologists have found high-quality bathtubs, often with a separate unit to store water. A person could sit in the bathtub while a slave drew water and poured it over the master's body. Many of these bathtubs fit against the wall like today's tubs and had seats and armrests.

Some bathrooms were divided into two areas, one for changing and one for washing. They were often built near the entrances of homes, suggesting that owners took baths and changed their clothes before entering the house.

Both bathtubs and water storage units were covered with a mixture of ashes, eggshells, and clay, which made them watertight. The same mixture was used to waterproof some **cisterns** for the collection of rain water—important in a country that was often dry. Besides collecting rain water, Carthaginians drew water from nearby springs and wells. When the Romans rebuilt Carthage, they added an aqueduct.

In addition to individual homes, archaeologists have found ruins of buildings that were six stories tall, similar to Rome's apartments. The walls of these buildings were made of stone, and the stairs of wood.

CARTHAGINIAN CLOTHING

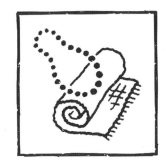

The Carthaginians mingled with many different populations, both in their travels and in their businesses at home. Because of this, their looks and clothing often varied. The examination of their bones shows that they were multiethnic, with a majority of African ancestry. They were small and slim, but strong.

Carthaginian artwork was not realistic, so it's difficult to determine popular clothing styles. They seem to have worn long, flowing tunics with long sleeves to shade and cool them in the North African heat.

In an ancient Roman play called *Poenulus* (The Young Carthaginian), a Greek man named Milphio teases a young stranger called Hanno about his clothing: "What bird is that, arriving here in the tunics? Was his cloak nabbed at the baths, I wonder?" Immediately, he guesses the visitor is from Carthage. To get his attention, he calls out, "Hey, you without a belt!"

The long tunic, worn by itself without a cloak or a belt, indicated his homeland. The "bird" might have been referring to the colors of the tunic, which were probably bright.

In most Carthaginian images, men and women had their heads covered, probably for protection from the sun. Some men wore full or partial turbans or conical hats. Women wore a cloth loosely wrapped around their heads. Feet were protected by sandals or boots.

Overall, Carthaginians didn't seem interested in showing off athletic bodies like the Greeks. Even their statues of gods and goddesses were clothed.

Cleanliness and Beauty

Besides bathing at home, the Carthaginians used public baths and scraped dirt and sweat off their bodies with strigils, like Greeks and Romans. They were famous perfume makers, and nearly every grave had a jar of scented oils or creams.

Apart from the clean-shaven priests, most men wore mustaches and beards. Women grew their hair long, usually parted in the middle. Greek hairstyles became fashionable near the end of Carthaginian civilization.

Jewelry

Jewels were popular in Carthage, as in most ancient cities. They included necklaces, **pendants**, bracelets, anklets, rings, and earrings for both men and women. Some types of jewelry indicated status or bravery. Armlets on Carthaginian warriors were like medals today: they received one for every campaign on which they served.

Earrings and nose rings were more common in Carthage than in other parts of the Mediterranean. In the *Poenulus*, the Greek Milthio

Be a Perfume Maker

The ancients used oils to make perfume, so they were subtle and could be detected only at a close distance. This activity will show you how they might have been made.

ADULT SUPERVISION REQUIRED

Materials

Large, fragrant rose (or other fragrant flower)

Mortar and pestle (or strong bowl and wooden spoon)

Saucepan

Water

Small glass containers with lids

Light oil such as olive, almond, or grape seed oil

6-by-5-inch cheesecloth

Small bowl

More roses, if needed

Adult helper

1. Pick the petals off a large, fragrant rose and place them in a mortar.

2. Fill a saucepan about a quarter of the way with water. Have an adult bring it to a boil on a stove.

3. While the water is heating, use a pestle to crush the petals in the mortar.

4. Place the crushed petals in a small glass container.

5. Pour oil into the container, just enough to cover the petals.

6. When the water boils, turn off the stove and ask an adult to place the container inside the saucepan.

7. Cover the container and leave it until the water cools.

8. Remove the container from the saucepan and leave it on a counter for 24 hours.

9. Remove the lid and place cheesecloth on top of the container. Slowly turn the full container over a small bowl so that the oil drains into it.

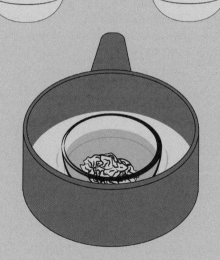

118

10. Gently wrap the cheesecloth around the flower petals so they all fit inside.

11. Twist and squeeze the cloth tightly to get every drop of oil.

12. Rub a little oil on your wrist and smell it. Can you detect a rose scent? If so, return the oil in the bowl to the glass container and keep it in a cool place. (Oil can get rancid.)

13. If the oil *doesn't* smell like roses, repeat every step with new rose petals, but use the same oil.

made fun of Hanno's servants who wore earrings. "I take it they have no fingers on their hands," he said.

Beads in the shape of men's faces were also common in Carthage. They had curly hair, beards, gold earrings, and large, staring eyes. The faces were painted white, red, yellow, blue, black, or green, regardless of the actual skin color. They may have been images of gods, to be worn for protection on necklaces or earrings.

Other jewelry showed popular symbols—birds, lions, lotus blossoms, and palmettes, which were worn for good luck. Some were shaped like gods or goddesses. Sometimes, Carthaginians hung metal boxes from their necks that contained tiny papyrus scrolls. On these scrolls they wrote special phrases or spells meant to keep away evil.

(left) **Carthaginian glass pendant from the fourth or third century BC.** Gift of J. Pierpont Morgan, 1917, to the Metropolitan Museum of Art, NY

(center) **Fifth-century glass pendant, with a face painted in turquoise-green.** Gift of Henry G. Marquand, 1881, to the Metropolitan Museum of Art, NY

(right) **Glass pendant from the third to the first century BC, hanging from an earring. The features on this face differ from others. It may have been a talisman used to scare away evil spirits.** The Cesnola Collection, purchased by subscription, 1874–76, Metropolitan Museum of Art, NY

Create a Carthaginian Pendant

Use the pictures on page119 to inspire the creation of a pendant to represent yourself or someone you know. You don't have to be realistic, not even in the colors. Just have fun!

Materials

Air-drying clay

Modeling tools

Small paper clip

Paintbrushes

Acrylic paint, different colors

1. Break off a piece of air-drying clay large enough to fit in the palm of your hand.

2. Knead it between your hands until it's soft and pliable.

3. Shape it into a face—someone you know, a favorite character from a book or movie, or a character from your imagination.

4. Use a modeling tool to sculpt the eyes and mouth. Shape the hair, nose, ears, beard, mustache, etc., with your fingers.

5. Insert a paper clip through the top of the head until only a small loop sticks out.

5. Leave it to dry.

6. Use paint to color the skin, hair, eyes, and lips.

7. Let it dry again.

8. Hang your creation as a room decoration. For example, a Santa Claus pendant can hang from a Christmas tree.

You can also make a smaller pendant by using half of the clay. It will be more difficult to shape, but it will be light enough to hang from a chain or leather strip around your neck.

CARTHAGINIAN WRITING

No Carthaginian writing survives in its original language, but there are Greek translations of some. One of the most interesting is a story called the *Periplus,* the adventures of a Carthaginian ruler named Hanno, who traveled along the Atlantic coast of North Africa with a large number of people. Their mission: to found new Carthaginian colonies.

Their trip was exciting and suspenseful. The lands they visited were unexplored, and the travelers didn't know what to expect. They saw elephants, hippopotami, and other wild animals. They admired tall mountains and fragrant and colorful trees. They met people who spoke languages they couldn't understand, and chased a band of hairy, stone-throwing creatures they called gorillas. No one today can determine what these creatures were; gorillas don't usually throw stones.

Some nights were frightful. Once, they saw fires and heard shouts and the sound of flutes and drums. On another night, along the coast, they observed "great torrents of fire [that] flowed down to the sea" and a flame so big that it "seemed to touch the stars." The next day, they realized it was a mountain—probably a volcano—called "Chariot of the Gods."

Through all this, the group started a colony in the location of today's Tangier, Morocco, and a few more along the same coast. From there, Hanno and some of the people moved farther south to explore more territory. Some historians believe he went around Africa, rather than returning to Carthage the same way.

The *Periplus* was written on tablets around the fifth century BC. They were dedicated to the god Melqart and placed in a temple. It is the longest known text by a Carthaginian author. It is also the first surviving report on northwest Africa.

Other Carthaginian books are known only by fame. For example, a book on agriculture written by retired general Hamilcar (not Hannibal's father) was well known at the time. The main authority on agriculture, however, was apparently another retired general, Mago, who wrote an encyclopedia on farming—28 volumes! This work has been destroyed, but enough survives in quotations by other authors to give an idea of Mago's suggestions to landowners. Apparently, he was one of the first to promote regular pruning of trees and the use of fertilizers for plants. He also advocated for better treatment of slaves.

CARTHAGINIAN ART AND MUSIC

Carthaginian art was greatly influenced by their trade and travels around the Mediterranean. They learned the techniques and styles of the Egyptians, Greeks, and Etruscans, and then produced their own distinctive art.

As with Etruscan art, most surviving Carthaginian artwork comes from tombs, so it is of a religious nature. One artist's name survives, Boethus the Carthaginian, who created some sculptures in Greece.

Sculpture

Today, most Carthaginian art is gone. Surviving works were made in stone or metal, which are strong and durable. The most common of these were the stelae, engraved blocks or stone tables that were common in the ancient world. Most of these stones were erected to the gods as reminders of requests or signs of gratitude for answered prayers. Some were found in graves, maybe as talismans or prayers for protection.

The most common symbols in stelae were circles representing the sun, moon crests, bottles, palms, temples, and open hands. There were also geometric shapes, especially triangles and hexagons. Historians still debate what these symbols meant. Since the open hand was found in many tombs, some think it was a stop sign to keep grave robbers away.

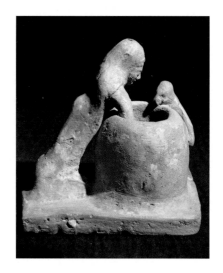

(left) **A Carthaginian stone with symbolic pictures. The image in the middle, with hands raised, is the typical representation of Tanit. Later she was represented more realistically, with a woman's features.** Erich Lessing / Art Resource, NY

(right) **Red terra-cotta figure showing a woman and child baking bread. Even if it's simple and stylized, it reveals many things about these two people and their close relationship.** Erich Lessing / Art Resource, NY

The goddess Tanit often appeared on stelae, either as a symbol (a circle over a triangle, separated by a horizontal rectangle or line) or, in later times, a realistic portrait. Images of priests performing sacrifices were also common. Some of these stelae show traces of paint, so they were probably colored.

Stone, and in rare cases marble, was also carved with inscriptions and small temples, which were placed above graves or on monuments. Small objects, such as figurines of gods and goddesses, incense burners, and daily objects, were made of bronze or less expensive terra-cotta.

One of the most common and popular Carthaginian exports were decorated ostrich eggs. Most ostriches came from the southern regions of Africa. They are fierce and dangerous but can be trained. Their eggs are normally as big as cantaloupes. Carthaginian artists would drain the eggs of their contents and paint them (usually red), using geometric forms, palms, lotus blossoms, or other common designs. These eggs were used as simple decorations or vases and often left in tombs as symbols of regeneration.

SYMBOLS

Over the centuries, people have used symbols to convey a particular thought or mental image, like emojis today. Ancient symbols, however, were often different than current ones. For example, few people today would use a picture of a horse to symbolize power, or a sheaf of wheat to symbolize abundance. Today, common symbols for power are a flexed arm, a raised fist, or an electric plug (depending on the type of power). For wealth, it's a money bag. On the other hand, the ancients wouldn't understand a heart as a symbol of love, because it wasn't used until the late Middle Ages.

Actual objects, such as a piece of clothing, a scepter, or a crown, could also be symbolic in ancient times. Many symbols associated with the gods were convenient and quick visual images. The symbol for the goddess Tanit was so easy to draw, anyone could quickly scratch it on a stone to invoke her help.

Ostrich egg, decorated with red paint. Album / Art Resource, NY

Make a Thanksgiving Stela

Stelae were often built to thank the gods for a received favor. What are some things that make you feel grateful? Make your own stela. If you celebrate Thanksgiving, you can do this as a family activity or class project.

Materials

Pencil

Paper or cardboard, 4¼-by-5½ inches

Scissors

½ pound of air-drying clay

Rolling pin

Cutting board

Modeling tools

Paintbrush

Acrylic paint

1. With a pencil and paper, draw a few things for which you are thankful. Arrange them so they touch and will be easy to cut out. Cut them out as one continuous piece.

2. Knead ⅔ of the air-drying clay with your hands, then use a rolling pin to flatten it on a cutting board. It should be about ½ inch thick.

3. Place your paper cutout on the clay and trace the outline using a modeling tool. Save the excess clay.

4. Now use scissors to cut out each image on the paper.

5. Place one of the cutout images on the clay, in the same position it appeared on the paper, then trace its outline with the modeling tool.

6. Remove the image and retrace the outline to make it visible. Lightly carve any details you may have in your drawing.

7. Repeat steps 5 and 6 for all the images.

8. Knead the leftover clay. Shape it into an oval, like a fat sausage.

9. Draw a line across the new shape with the modeling tool, opening a ½-inch-wide slit.

10. Insert the stela into the slit and press down to make it as stable as possible.

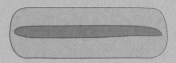

11. Lean it against a support and let dry.

12. Once dry, paint it.

13. After the paint dries, you can use it as placeholder for a Thanksgiving meal or keep it as a reminder of the good things in your life.

COINS OF CARTHAGE

Coins are often counted among the Carthaginians' finest artistic works, even if they were not made for that purpose. Common designs include a horse's head, a full horse, a lion in front of a palm tree, a single palm tree, the god Melqart with a club on his shoulder, a female goddess, a war elephant, and the prow of a warship. The coins were made of silver, gold, and bronze.

Silver Carthaginian coin, minted in Sicily in the fourth century BC. On one side is a galloping horse ridden by the Greek goddess Nike, who symbolized victory. On the other side, a palm tree with the writing MHNT, meaning "the army." Classical Numismatic Group

Music

Archaeologists have found Carthaginian images of girls playing double flutes and tambourines, and gods or goddesses playing harps or small guitars. Because Carthaginians had a reputation for being serious and practical, with little time for fun, historians have concluded their music was mainly for religious purposes.

Create and Play a Carthaginian Tambourine

Tambourines were very popular in the ancient world. Make a small one to tap to the beat of your favorite songs.

Materials

Container of spreadable cheese wedges, emptied

Large paintbrush

White or yellow acrylic paint

Roll of 1-inch-wide masking tape (any color)

Hole punch

Pipe cleaners

Small jingle bells

1. Empty a spreadable cheese wedge container and discard one half—or give it to a friend for their own tambourine.

2. Paint colors onto each side. If the label is still visible, let the paint dry and apply a new coat. (Wash the paintbrush between coats.)

3. Wrap masking tape around the container until the whole edge is covered.

4. Use the hold punch to add holes an inch apart around the taped edge.

5. Wire a pipe cleaner through each hole and through the hook of jingle bell. Twist the stem to secure.

4. Hold it with one hand and tap on one side with the other hand make music.

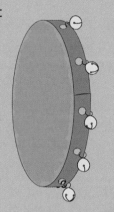

Baal Marqod was a Phoenician and Carthaginian god whose name meant "lord of the dance," so the Carthaginians must have danced during religious worship. These may have been somber and slow dances, like some Greek dances today, or wild and frenzied to wake up the gods.

Like the other nations around them, the Carthaginians used trumpets and horns before battle to inspire the soldiers and scare the enemy.

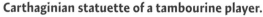

Carthaginian statuette of a tambourine player.
Erich Lessing / Art Resource, NY

CARTHAGINIAN RELIGION

Most of Carthage's gods and goddesses had been worshiped by the Phoenicians, but some were purely Carthaginian. The name Baal means "lord," so it was attached to different qualities to indicate different gods. Baal Hammon (its name's meaning is unclear) became the main god in Carthage. Lesser gods included Melqart (chief god of the Phoenician city of Tyre) and Eshmun (chief god of the Phoenician city of Sidon). Traditionally, Baal's female companion was Astarte, but in Carthage Tanit was more important.

To pacify the gods in difficult times, or to ask for special favors, Carthaginians sacrificed animals. Most historians believe they also sacrificed young children. Historians base this conviction on writings by ancient Greeks and Romans and on some archaeological findings. For example, in a burial place named Tophet, near Carthage, archaeologists have discovered tens of thousands of urns with the cremated bones of infants.

By itself, the fact that many babies were buried in one place doesn't prove they had been sacrificed. Babies could have simply been buried in a separate area of town. However, a Carthaginian stone image of a priest holding a child seems to confirm this practice, which was common among other populations at that time. Many ancients thought that if the gods were angry, this ultimate sacrifice would be a sign of the people's devotion.

(left) **A cemetery for Carthaginian children. It is commonly known as Tophet, from a name used in the Bible.** Giraud Patrick, Wikimedia Commons

(right) **Carthaginian grinning mask made of baked clay in the sixth century BC.** HIP/Art Resource, NY

ACTIVITY

Mass-Produce Some Figurines

As other populations around them, the Carthaginians produced little statues of gods and goddesses. They made them inexpensively through mass production. To mass-produce statues, they used one mold for each god or goddess and added details such as outstretched arms later.

Materials

Small figurine

½ pound terra-cotta modeling clay

Modeling tool

Paintbrush

Paints

1. Choose a simple figurine, without many details.

2. Take half of the terra-cotta, knead it, and shape into an egg. It should be a little bigger than your figurine. (Keep the other piece of terra-cotta wrapped.)

3. Using a modeling tool, cut the terra-cotta egg in half lengthwise.

4. Push the figurine halfway into one of the halves.

5. Place the other half onto the figurine and press until the two halves meet.

6. Gently reopen the halves and remove the figurine. You will see two molds.

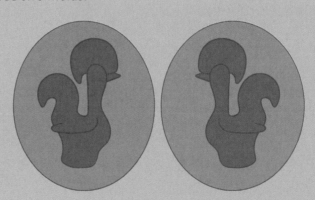

7. Let the two halves dry completely.

8. When they are dry, knead another piece of terra-cotta dough.

9. Place the piece in one mold. Cover it with the other mold and press firmly.

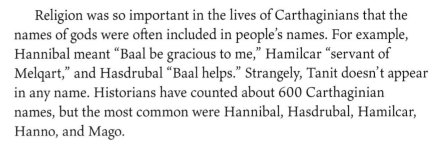

10. Gently open the molds.

11. Use the modeling tool to take off any extra dough from the edges of your new figurine.

12. Touch up the details of your figurine—eyes, mouth, nose, and ears.

13. Let your figurine dry.

14. Paint it to match your initial figurine.

15. Repeat as many times as you like to make more figurines.

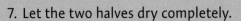

Religion was so important in the lives of Carthaginians that the names of gods were often included in people's names. For example, Hannibal meant "Baal be gracious to me," Hamilcar "servant of Melqart," and Hasdrubal "Baal helps." Strangely, Tanit doesn't appear in any name. Historians have counted about 600 Carthaginian names, but the most common were Hannibal, Hasdrubal, Hamilcar, Hanno, and Mago.

ACTIVITY

Scare Off Evil Spirits with a Carthaginian Mask

While digging inside Carthaginian tombs, archaeologists have found many small face masks. These masks have large open mouths and empty eyes. Some have large ears. They can be grinning or frowning. Because they are too small to be worn, some historians believe they were left in the tombs or hung on walls to scare off evil spirits. Try making a similar mask.

Materials

¼ pound air-drying clay (white or red)

Rolling pin

Modeling tools

Balloon

Paintbrush and paints (optional)

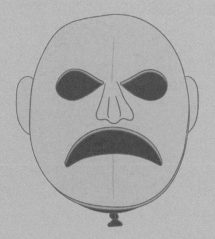

1. Knead air-drying clay with your hands until it's soft.

2. Lay it on a clean working surface and flatten it with a rolling pin.

3. Cut out a 6-inch square using a modeling tool. Keep the leftover pieces of clay.

4. Use the modeling tool to draw a light line in the middle of the square, from top to bottom. With the tool, draw a large eye on each side of the line and a large mouth underneath. The mouth can be smiling or frowning.

5. With the same modeling tool, retrace the lines of the eyes and mouth until you cut them out. Keep the pieces.

6. Round off the edges of the square with the modeling tool.

7. Blow up the balloon until it's as big as a man's hand.

8. Gently remove the mask from the table and push it against the balloon to make it round.

9. Use the leftover pieces of clay to make a nose and two ears and attach them to the mask.

10. Let the mask dry.

11. Color it if you like.

CARTHAGINIAN GOVERNMENT AND WARFARE

In the beginning, Carthage was a monarchy like most nations around it. By the third century BC, it became a republic, ruled by representatives of the wealthy class. Wealth was considered equal to merit, if not more important, because the poor don't have time to rule.

In the republic, most decisions were made by two leaders, known as *sufetes*, who were elected and had to collaborate with a group of 300 counselors called *adirim* (the mighty ones).

If the *sufetes* and the *adirim* could not agree, decisions were taken to the people, who were called to the city square. In some cases, the people made crucial decisions. In 241 BC, when Carthage's mercenary soldiers and the conquered people of North Africa banded together in rebellion against Carthage, it was the frightened people who chose as their general Hamilcar Barca, father of Hannibal. Both of these men changed the course of Carthage's history.

The full details of this republican government are not clear, but the Greek philosopher Aristotle praised it as a model of balanced rule, a mixture of monarchy (since the *sufetes* were above the people), aristocracy (rule of a few), and democracy (rule of the people). Aristotle also admired the constitution of Carthage, which had "many outstanding features as compared with those of other nations."

It was a high praise, because the Greeks despised any population besides their own (except Egypt). But Aristotle was not talking about his personal preference. "A proof of a well-regulated constitution," he said, lies in the fact that the people "willingly remain faithful to the constitutional system, and that neither civil strife has arisen in any degree worth mentioning, nor yet a tyrant." This was the case with Carthage.

As in Rome, officers ran different government agencies. Ten men were in charge of building and maintaining sacred places, and a group of 30 made sure everyone paid their taxes. A council of 100 judges, chosen from the *adirim,* were in charge of judging the generals and the military. This council prevented a general from taking over the government. When a general returned from war, these judges would ask for a detailed account of what happened and make sure it was in accordance with the constitution.

They were extremely strict. When the Romans defeated a Carthaginian general named Hanno, the council of judges found him at fault and condemned him to death by crucifixion. These judges were so cruel, some generals committed suicide rather than be handed over to them.

Carthaginian Warfare

Though Carthage had brilliant generals and admirals, most of its troops were foreign soldiers. This allowed the Carthaginians to protects the lives of their citizens and to pick professional fighters. Lybians were disciplined and organized in battle, preferring close combat with long thrusting spears, while the Celts, Celtiberians, and Numidians were famous for their horse-riding skills and could launch a tempest of javelins on the enemy. A good general knew how to use these skills efficiently. Some foreign soldiers (such as the Celts) made excellent partners because they also wanted to bring down Rome's government.

Many military positions were occupied by Carthaginians. Generals and admirals were from Carthage, and many of the rowers in the boats were poor Carthaginians in need of work.

Using foreign soldiers had disadvantages, too, especially if they fought for money. When pay didn't arrive on time, they didn't hesitate to turn violent against Carthage.

Most historians agree that the Carthaginians' attitude to war had much to do with their final destruction. They expected wars to end in peace treaties, with the losing nation giving land and money to the winner. When the Romans threatened them, they looked for a compromise. But the Romans expected to fight to the finish—total victory or their own destruction. Many Carthaginian senators left the military work to the generals and didn't fight until the very end, even when the Romans were at their doors.

WEAPONS OF CARTHAGE

The Carthaginian army did not have a uniform suit of armor. Each soldier used what he could afford. Some fought without any armor, while others purchased beautiful sculpted armor with images of gods or other patriotic symbols.

The type of armor and equipment also depended on the nationality of the soldiers. The Numidians rode their horses without bridles or saddles, and most soldiers from European tribes fought without armor.

CARTHAGINIAN DAILY LIFE

Carthage was built as a colony of traders. The military existed to create new trading colonies and defend existing territories. Artisans and farmers produced goods for both national and international consumption. Sometimes growing and trading went hand in hand, and many merchants owned large farms.

Merchants and Explorers

Like Hanno, who traveled the coast of Africa, Himilco was a famous Carthaginian explorer. He followed the Atlantic coast from Spain to northern France and visited islands between Spain and England. Himilco described one island that was inhabited by menacing people wearing black tunics and cloaks hanging all the way to their feet, who walked around with canes. To him, they looked like the goddesses of vengeance in Greek tragedies.

Himilco talked of terrible dangers he faced on his trips, including frightening sea monsters. Some think he told those stories to scare other merchants from following the routes he took to natural sources of tin and lead. Merchants also used drastic measures to protect their trade routes. Strabo wrote about a ship captain who ran his ship ashore, losing all his crew and barely escaping, rather than lead a Roman ship behind him to natural deposits of tin. When he returned home, Carthaginian authorities rewarded him.

Besides scouring the Atlantic coast, some Carthaginian explorers crossed the Sahara Desert to West Africa, where they found precious gold, ivory, ebony, and wild animals and their skins or hides. Wild animals were in great demand in Rome, where they were used in gladiatorial games. Rich people also liked to impress guests with at least one wild pet. Desert travel was difficult but worth the risk.

Once a trade route was established, merchants followed it regularly to buy and sell their products, and the local populations awaited them with great anticipation. According to the Greek historian Herodotus, when Carthaginian merchants landed near a city, they would place their goods on shore, go back on the ship, and create smoke signals to attract customers. Locals would soon arrive with silver and gold. If they could agree on a price, the Carthaginians sold their goods and left. Otherwise, they waited until the people raised their offers.

Farmers

Carthaginian farmers raised grains such as wheat and barley, vegetables, lentils, beans, fruit, and some nuts, such as almonds and pistachios. Pomegranates were so common the Romans called them *malum punicum* (Punic apples). Grapes were also abundant, and Carthaginian wine was sold in many nations, especially a sweet wine made from raisins.

Olives were another important crop. They were cured and eaten whole or crushed for their oil, which was used in kitchens, baths (instead of soap), and as fuel for lamps.

Carthaginians were experts at pruning, and they used an effective threshing machine the Romans called *plostellum punicum*—a roller with razors—which cut wheat when pulled over a field. They also became known for their irrigation methods, which helped them to grow crops even in some desert areas.

Carthaginians also kept bees for both honey and beeswax, and raised cattle, sheep, goats, pigs, chicken, horses, donkeys, and mules. Along the coast, fishermen caught great quantities of fish that were eaten whole or fermented to make *garum* sauce. Some collected murex shells, which were then processed to produce expensive purple dye.

The Greek historian Diodorus explains how a fruitful region near Carthage was "divided into gardens and plantations of every kind, since many streams of water were led in small channels and irrigated every part." He also said, "Part of the land was planted with vines, and part yielded olives and was also planted thickly with other varieties of fruit-bearing trees. On each side herds of cattle and flocks of sheep pastured on the plain, and the neighboring meadows were filled with grazing horses."

Diodorus attributed the abundance of the area to "the leading Carthaginians [who] had laid out there their private estates and with their wealth had beautified them for their enjoyment," so much that their homes were stocked with all kinds of goods. Many of these Carthaginians were retired generals and merchants. In their search for enjoyment and prosperity, they used the skills they had acquired in their careers to turn the region of Carthage into productive land.

Artisans

The Carthaginians also created beautiful pottery, fine textiles, and exceptional perfumes. Artisans were also experts at working glass, wood, alabaster, ivory, bronze, gold, silver, and precious stones.

Polybius wrote that when Scipio Africanus captured New Carthage, Spain, in 209 BC, he took 10,000 prisoners, which included both citizens and 2,000 artisans (or craftsmen). The citizens were given immediate freedom, which they could keep as long as they stayed loyal to Rome. But the artisans were considered slaves of Rome, with the possibility of being freed at the end of the war against Carthage. Of the others (probably slaves), he took the strongest for the Roman navy, again promising freedom. This might explain why many artisans in Carthage (as well as New Carthage) were either free immigrants or slaves.

Family Life

The Carthaginians didn't leave records of their family lives, but their families functioned much like those in nations around them. Children played with toys and pets until a certain age. Being close to Africa, some might have had pet monkeys. In the *Poenulus*, Hanno recognized his nephew by a bite mark left by a pet monkey when the boy was young.

At a certain age, usually around seven, children put away their toys to devote time to their studies or practical lessons, following in their parents' footsteps. Wealthy families gave their children thorough educations, like the Greeks. Hannibal had a Greek tutor and probably learned to appreciate the Greek classics, such as Homer's epic poems. These books taught children to be brave and resourceful, two important virtues at the time.

Even though Carthage was founded by a queen, Carthaginian women had very limited roles in society. They were not granted citizenship and could not participate in the city's decisions. When the government called an assembly of the people for advice, it meant only men.

Women did, however, sacrifice for their country, working alongside men and donating their goods, as well as running the household and parts of their husbands' businesses while the men were traveling or at war. Hannibal's father, Hamilcar, was away from Carthage much of the time, but the number of children he had with his wife shows he returned home for visits to rest and enjoy his family.

Once, the Carthaginian government asked the troops to take their families to the battlefield, thinking that the men would be more motivated to stay. It was a colossal failure because there were too many mouths to feed.

CARTHAGINIAN FOOD

As in most Mediterranean countries, Carthaginian meals were joyful occasions. They were usually eaten at home, but sometimes they were social occasions or important meetings. The men of Carthage belonged to different clubs related to their occupations, which would normally meet around a table. Hannibal held some of his diplomatic meetings during meals.

Few Carthaginian recipes have survived. Mago, the author of books on agriculture, described how Carthaginians made flour: they soaked wheat (or barley) in plenty of water, pounded it with a pestle, dried it in the sun, and then pounded it again. Most ancient populations pounded the dry grain immediately, but soaking it first made the process easier and might have prevented hard kernels from scraping the stone. Accidentally mixing stone grit with the flour was a common and painful problem, because the grit scratched tooth enamel and caused dental problems.

Mago left a recipe for Carthaginian raisin wine that even their enemies in Rome loved. It was a long process of soaking sun-dried raisins in the best unfermented wine, squeezing out the liquid, repeating the process, and leaving the final wine to ferment. Dry fruit was very popular in Carthage and most Mediterranean countries because it was easy to make and lasted a long time.

Fill Up with Hearty Carthaginian Grains

A Carthaginian recipe for puls punica *has survived in a book on agriculture written by the Roman general Marcus Porcius Cato: "Soak one pound of farro [a type of wheat] in water until it's soft. Pour it into a clean bowl, add three pounds of fresh cheese, half a pound of honey, and one egg. Mix well and place it into a new pot." To Italians,* puls punica *sounds like a dessert from Naples, Italy, called* pastiera. *This activity follows a similar process. The recipe has been modified, because the ancients liked their food sweeter than we do. You can substitute farro with wheat, but you should cook it for a short time (preferably in milk) after soaking, then wait until it cools.*

ADULT SUPERVISION REQUIRED

Materials

Mixing bowl

½ cup farro kernels

1 cup water

Strainer

Oven

2 eggs

2 cups fresh ricotta cheese

4 tablespoons honey

10-inch round cake pan or premade pie crust

2 serving bowls

1. In a mixing bowl, soak the farro kernels in water overnight.

2. Use a strainer to drain the kernels.

3. Preheat the oven to 350 degrees Fahrenheit.

4. Rinse the bowl, return the kernels to the bowl, crack two eggs into it, then add ricotta and honey.

5. Mix well, then pour the mixture into the pan (or pie crust).

6. Bake 1 hour or until the top is golden.

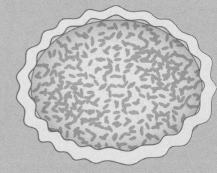

As an alternative, you can blend the farro grains after they have been soaked and strained. Or you can use cupcake liners and make small muffins. In this case, bake 15 minutes (or until golden).

GLOSSARY

altar Platform used for offering sacrifices.

amber Tree resin that has hardened over time. Amber jewelry was thought to have magical powers.

amphitheater An oval or circular building with seats arranged around an open space.

anklet Jewelry that is worn around the ankle.

aqueduct A bridge-like structure used to carry water from one place to another.

arch Curved part of a structure that is used for ornament and support.

archaeologist Scientist who studies ancient objects to determine how their owners lived.

augures Singular: augur. In ancient Etruria and Rome, religious officials who interpreted the will of the gods by observing natural signs, especially the behavior of birds.

barbarian A person from another country who is believed to be less civilized.

battering ram A heavy beam with an iron tip that was swung back and forth against a wall or door to knock it down.

bog Wet, spongy ground.

brazier Pan for holding burning coals.

brooch Jewelry with a pin used to hold clothes together in ancient times.

bust Sculpture of a person's head, neck, and at least part of the shoulders.

cargo Goods carried by plane, ship, or vehicle.

cavalry An army unit of soldiers on horses.

cauldron Large pot.

century A company in the ancient Roman army, composed of 80–100 men.

cistern Underground tank for storing water.

civil war War between people of the same country.

colony Distant territory belonging to another nation.

consul One of two top Roman government officers who held power together for a year.

courtyard Open area in the middle of a building or next to it.

cremate Burn to ashes, often a dead body.

cuirass Armor that protects a soldier from the neck to the waist.

dagger Short knife used as a weapon.

decipher To interpret into a familiar language.

dictator In republican Rome, a leader who, in an emergency, had absolute power for six months.

diplomacy The skill of dealing with others and resolving conflicts through peaceful discussion.

divination Religious practice of using signs to predict the future.

edile Government officer responsible for day-to-day aspects of city life.

emperor In ancient Rome, a commander. Later, a ruler over a large territory.

empire Large territory ruled by an emperor or empress.

fresco Artistic painting on fresh plaster.

fulguratores Singular: fulgurator. In ancient Etruria and Rome, religious officials who interpreted the will of the gods by observing lightning in the sky.

garum Sauce made from fermented fish products.

gladiator In ancient Rome, a trained fighter for public entertainment.

governor Ruler of a Roman province.

haruspices Singular: haruspex. In ancient Etruria and Rome, religious officials who interpreted the will of the gods by observing the insides of animals.

infantry Army unit of soldiers who fight on foot.

inscription Words written or engraved as a permanent record.

jet Coal polished as a gemstone. Jet jewelry was thought to have magical powers.

legion Military unit, with a varying number of soldiers. At the time of Augustus, it had 4,800 men.

legionnaire Soldier in a legion.

lime Product of limestone, used to make cement.

limestone Rock made mostly of calcium.

linen Cloth made from the long fibers of the flax plant.

loft Living or storage space just below the roof of a building.

loom Frame used for weaving cloth.

lyre U-shaped stringed instrument, similar to a small harp.

mail Protective armor made by small, linked metal rings.

mausoleum Large tomb.

mercenary Soldier who is hired to fight.

monarchy Type of government where a king or queen rules over the people.

mortar Strong, deep bowl in which materials are ground with a pestle.

mosaic Artwork made by joining together small pieces of colored material.

mythology Traditional stories of a particular culture.

papyrus Tall reed that grows abundantly in Egypt; the central part of papyrus stems were used to make ancient paper.

patron Generous supporter.

pendant Ornament that hangs down.

pestle Hard tool with a rounded head, used to grind material in a mortar.

philosopher Someone who studies and discusses the meaning of life.

pope Initially, a title given to any important bishop in the Christian church; later used for the leader of the Roman Catholic Church.

Principate The first four centuries of the Roman Empire.

quarry Place where stones are extracted from the earth.

questor Roman government officer with financial duties.

quinquereme Large ship with about 300 men, divided in groups of five.

relief Sculpture in which figures are only partially raised from the background.

republic Government ruled by elected representatives.

resin Substance obtained from the gum or sap of some trees.

satire Speech or writing meant to make fun of or show the weaknesses of a person or situation.

scribe Person trained in writing or copying documents.

siege The act of an army surrounding a fortified place to prevent it from receiving help and supplies, forcing it to surrender.

spindle Rod or stick used to wind thread or yarn while spinning.

strigil Curved metal instrument used by Romans to scrape dirt off skin.

stylized Simple image style used to represent a subject, rather than a realistic image.

talisman Object believed to have magical powers.

tavern Place that provides food and beds to travelers.

terra-cotta Reddish clay used for statues, plates, and pots, or as building material.

toga Long cloth worn by Roman citizens, wrapped around their bodies for formal occasions.

tufa Volcanic stone.

tunic Garment similar to a long T-shirt.

tributary Stream of water that joins a larger stream.

woad Plant grown for the blue dye extracted from its leaves.

ACKNOWLEDGMENTS

I am grateful for all the people who have come by my side on this long journey through ancient lands, starting with Lisa Reardon, former editor at Chicago Review Press, who steered me in the right direction when I was trying to decide on a new book to write; Jerome Pohlen, who has enthusiastically picked up this project; and Ellen Hornor, who has carefully edited it.

I owe a great debt of gratitude to Prof. Sir Barry Cunliffe, emeritus professor of European archaeology at the University of Oxford, for taking time out of his busy schedule to graciously answer some questions on the Celts, and to Prof. David Noe, associate professor of classics at Calvin College, for his careful reading of the manuscript, his valuable suggestions, and his corrections of my Latin translations.

I am also thankful for my friend Ellie Charter, who has listened to a reading of portions of this book and has helped me to refine some of the activities, and for my husband and children who have patiently walked around boxes of craft supplies.

RESOURCES

Books

Books on Ancient Rome: History and Culture

Bonaventura, Maria Antonietta Lozzi. *Pompeii Reconstructed*. Rome, Italy: Archeolibri, 2007.

Butterfield, Moira. *Going to War in Roman Times*. London, UK: Franklin Watt, 2001.

Goldsworthy, Adrian. *The Complete Roman Army*. London, UK: Thames & Hudson, 2003.

James, Simon. *Ancient Rome*. New York: DK, 2008.

Books on Ancient Rome: Activity Books

Carlson, Laurie. *Classical Kids: An Activity Guide to Life in Ancient Greece and Rome*. Chicago: Chicago Review Press, 1998.

Hanson-Harding, Alexandra. *Ancient Rome*. New York: Scholastic, 2000.

Guides on Visiting Rome

Family Guide Rome. New York: DK Eyewitness Travel, 2017.

Pasquesi, J. M. *Rome with Kids, an Insider's Guide*. Chicago: Solo Roma Books, 2014.

Books on the Etruscans

Morris, Neil, Matteo Chesi, Antonella, Paola Ravaglia, and Marco Nardi. *The Etruscans* (Back to Basics). Florence, Italy: McRAE Books, 2009.

Guides on Visiting Etruria

Italia Etrusca, Guida Completa. Florence, Italy: Guide Giunti, 2000. Unfortunately, this book has not been translated into English, but it is still a good buy for the images, maps, names of cities, museums, restaurants, hotels, etc.

Travel Guide Italy. New York: DK Eyewitness, 2016.

Books on the Celts

Burnett, Allan. *The Celts and All That*. Edinburgh, UK: Birlin, 2016.

Goscinny, Renée. *Asterix the Gaul*. London, UK: Orion, 2004. The first of a fun series of comic books.

Green, Jen. *Ancient Celts: Archaeology Unlocks the Secrets of the Celts' Past*. Washington, DC: National Geographic Children's Books, 2008.

Taylor, Dereen. *Celts*. New York: Powerkids, 2010.

Books on the Carthaginians

Brooks, Philip. *Hannibal: Rome's Worst Nightmare*. New York: Scholastic, 2009.

Gerrard, Mike. *Travel Guide: Tunisia*. New York: DK Eyewitness Travel, 2011.

Salimbet, Andrea, and Raffaele D'Amato. *The Carthaginians, 6th–2nd Century BC*. New York: Osprey, 2014.

Sean Stewart Price. *Hannibal of Carthage*. Chicago: Raintree Books, 2014.

Warrick, Karen Clemens. *Hannibal: Great General of the Ancient World*. Berkley Heights, NY: Enslow, 2006.

Online Videos and Websites

The Ancient Romans

Cassel, Christopher, dir. *Rome: Engineering an Empire*. The History Channel, 2005.

Garland, Robert. *A Day in the Life of a Roman Soldier*. TedEd. https://ed.ted.com/lessons/a-day-in-the-life-of-a-roman-soldier-robert-garland.

Laurence, Ray. *A Glimpse of Teenage Life in Ancient Rome*. TedEd. https://ed.ted.com/lessons/a-glimpse-of-teenage-life-in-ancient-rome-ray-laurence.

Laurence, Ray. *Four Sisters in Ancient Rome*. TedEd. https://ed.ted.com/lessons/four-sisters-in-ancient-rome-ray-laurence.

PBS. The Roman Empire in the First Century. http://www.pbs.org/empires/romans.

The Etruscans

Ministry of Cultural Heritage and Activities and Tourism. Experience Etruria. http://www.experiencetruria.it/en/node/31.

Servizio Musei e Beni Culturali. *The Dawn of the Etruscans*. Media Vision, 2016. https://www.youtube.com/watch?v=1akolRC02vw.

The Celts

Iron Age Celts. http://www.bbc.co.uk/wales/celts/index.shtml?1.

The Carthaginians

Cannon, Mark, dir. *Engineering an Empire: Carthage*. The History Channel, 2006.

Hufnail, Mark, dir. *The True Story of Hannibal*. The History Channel, 2005.

NOTES

When the reference is to a Latin source, the translation was the author's.

"Tullius to his wife Terentia": Cicero, *Epistulae Ad Familiares* XIV, VIII.

"Hey, you who are passing": Frédéric Edouard Plessis, *Éptaphes; textes choisis et commentaires publies* (Paris: A. Fontemoing, 1905), 117. https://archive.org/details/ptaphes textesc00plesuoft.

"I lived as I wanted": Dessau Hermannus, *Inscriptiones Latinae Selectae* (Berlin: Apud Weimannos, 1906), 882.

"Here is buried Leburna": Hermannus, *Inscriptiones*, 326.

"Gaius Julius Polybius for edile": Brian K. Harvey, *Daily Life in Ancient Rome: A Sourcebook* (Indianapolis, IN: Hackett, 2016), 145.

"The late-night drinkers": Harvey, *Daily Life*, 145.

"If you deliberately": Gregory S. Aldrete, *Daily Life in the Roman City: Rome, Pompeii and Ostia* (Westport, CT: Greenwood, 2004), 232.

"none is better": Cicero, *De Officiis*, Loeb Classical Library, 1913, Book I, 42:151, http://penelope.uchicago.edu/Thayer/E/Roman/Texts/Cicero/de_Officiis/1E*.html

"Don't you know?": Plutarch, *Parallel Lives, Life of Lucullus*, 41:2 (modified by author).

"with rippling muscles": Diodorus Siculus, *The Library of History*, Loeb Classical Library edition, Vol. III, Book V (Cambridge, MA: Harvard University Press, 1939), 28.

"very tall": Cassius Dio, *Roman History*, 42:2.4, Loeb Classical Library, Vol. VIII (Cambridge, MA: Harvard University Press, 1925).

"The stone protects": Julius Caesar, *De bello Gallico*, Book 7, chapter 23, trans. W. A. McDevitte and W. S. Bohn (London: Bell, 1918).

"striking": Diodorus Siculus, *The Library of History*, Loeb Classical Library, Vol. III, Book V (Cambridge, MA: Harvard University Press, 1939), 30:1.

"heavy for winter": Siculus, *Library of History*, 30:1.

"Some of them shave": Siculus, *Library of History*, 28.3.

"When they are eating": Siculus, *Library of History*, 28.3.

"the standard measure": Strabo, *Geography*, Loeb Classical Library, Vol. II, Book IV (Cambridge, MA: Harvard University Press, 1923), 137.

"to gallop their teams": Julius Caesar*, The Gallic War*, Loeb Classical Library, Book IV (Cambridge, MA: Harvard University Press, 1917), 33.

"he placed huge cauldrons": Athenaeus, *The Deipnosophists*, Book 4, trans. C. D.Yonge, 1854, http://www.attalus.org/info/athenaeus.html.

"planted with gardens": Appian, *The Punic Wars*, trans. Horace White (New York: Macmillan, 1899), 24:117.

"What bird is that": Plautus, *The Little Carthaginian*, trans. Paul Nixon (London: William Heinemann, 1916), 99.

"Hey, you without": Plautus, *Little Carthaginian*, 101.

"I take it they have": Plautus, *Little Carthaginian*, 99.

"great torrents": Hanno, *The Periplus*, trans. Wilfred H. Schoff (Philadelphia: Commercial Museum, 1912), par. 15.

"many outstanding features": Aristotle, *Politics*, in *Aristotle in 23 Volumes*, Vol. 21, trans. H. Rackham (London: William Heinemann, 1944), 2.1272b.

"A proof": Aristotle, *Politics*.

"divided into gardens": Diodorus Siculus, *The Library of History*, Vol. X, Book XX, Loeb Classical Library edition, (Cambridge, MA: Harvard University Press, 1954), par. 8:3–4.

"Soak one pound": Marcus Porcius Cato, *De Re Rustica*, Chapters 74–90, par. 85, (London: Loeb Classical Library, 1934).

Selected Bibliography

The Romans

Angela, Alberto. *A Day in the Life of Ancient Rome: Daily Life, Mysteries, and Curiosities.* Translated by Gregory Conti. New York: Europa Editions, 2009.

Angela, Alberto. *The Reach of Rome: A Journey Through the Lands of the Ancient Empire, Following a Coin.* Translated by Gregory Conti. New York: Rizzoli Ex Libris, 2013.

Beard, Mary. *SPQR: A History of Ancient Rome.* New York: Liveright, 2016.

Cunliffe, Barry. *Rome and the Barbarians.* London, UK: Bodley Head, Penguin Books, 1975.

Goldsworthy, Adrian. *The Complete Roman Army,* London, UK: Thames & Hudson, 2003.

Goldsworthy, Adrian. *Augustus, First Emperor of Rome.* New Haven, CT: Yale University Press, 2014.

Goldsworthy, Adrian. *Caesar, Life of a Colossus.* New Haven, CT: Yale University Press, 2008.

Goldsworthy, Adrian. *How Rome Fell: Death of a Superpower.* New Haven, CT: Yale University Press, 2010.

Goldsworthy, Adrian. *Pax Romana.* New Haven, CT: Yale University Press, 2016.

Harl, Kenneth W. *Rome and the Barbarians.* Chantilly, VA: Teaching Company, 2004.

Harvey, Brian K. *Daily Life in Ancient Rome: A Sourcebook.* Indianapolis, IN: Hackett, 2016.

The Etruscans

Bonfante, Larissa. *Etruscan Dress.* Baltimore: Johns Hopkins University Press, 2003.

Bonfante, Larissa. *Etruscan Myths.* Austin: University of Texas Press, 2006.

Bonfante, Larissa. *Etruscan* (Reading the Past*).* Berkeley: University of California Press, 1990.

Smith, Christopher. *The Etruscans: A Very Short Introduction.* Oxford, UK: Oxford University Press, 2014.

Tuck, Steven L. *The Mysterious Etruscans.* Indianapolis, IN: Teaching Company, 2016.

The Celts

Cunliffe, Barry. *The Ancient Celts.* New York: Penguin, 1999.

Cunliffe, Barry. *Druids: A Very Short Introduction.* Oxford, UK: Oxford University Press, 2010.

Ellis, Peter Berresford. *Brief History of the Celts.* London, UK: Robinson, 2003.

Freeman, Phillip. *The Philosopher and the Druids: A Journey Among the Ancient Celts.* New York: Simon and Schuster, 2008.

Paxton, Jennifer. *The Celtic World.* Indianapolis, IN: Teaching Company, 2018.

Stead, Ian Matheson. *Celtic Art: In Britain Before the Roman Conquest.* London, UK: British Museum Press, 1996.

The Carthaginians

Charles-Picard, Gilbert, and Colette Charles-Picard. *Daily Life in Carthage*. New York: Macmillan, 1968.

Hoyos, Dexter. *The Carthaginians*. New York: Routledge, 2010.

Hunt, Patrick. *Hannibal*. New York: Simon and Schuster, 2017.

Ancient Works Cited

Aristotle. *Politics*. Translated by H. Rackham. http://www.perseus.tufts.edu/hopper.

Cassius Dio. *Roman History*. http://penelope.uchicago.edu/Thayer/E/Roman/home.html.

Cicero. *Epistulae Ad Familiares*. http://www.thelatinlibrary.com.

Diodorus Siculus. *The Library of History*. http://penelope.uchicago.edu/Thayer/E/Roman/home.html.

Hanno. *The Periplus*. Translated by Wilfred H. Schoff. https://archive.org/details/cu31924031441847/page/n1.

Julius Caesar. *De bello Gallico*. Translated by W. A. McDevitte and W. S. Bohn. http://classics.mit.edu/Browse/index.html.

Julius Caesar. *The Gallic War*. http://penelope.uchicago.edu/Thayer/E/Roman/home.html.

Marcus Porcius Cato. *De Re Rustica*. http://penelope.uchicago.edu/Thayer/E/Roman/home.html.

Plutarch. *Parallel Lives, Life of Lucullus*. http://penelope.uchicago.edu/Thayer/E/Roman/home.html.

INDEX

T

Tacitus
on Caractacus, 76
on Roman/Druids battle, 95
on Roman self-indulgence, 77
Tagetes, 65
Tagetic Books, 65
talismans, 82
Tanaquil, 50
Tanit, *122*, 123, 127, 129
Taranis, 94
Tarcontes, 65
Tarquinia, 45, 48
Tarquinius Superbus, 3, 44
tebenna, 50
temples
Carthaginian, 115
Egyptian, 115
Etruscan, 14, 49
Greek, 14, 49
Roman, 8, 14, 22, 34
terra-cotta, 62
Tertullian, 113
testudo formation, *32*
Thalna, 63
Thesan, 63
Thornycroft, Thomas, 77
Tiber River, 2
Ticino River, 19
Timaeus, on Celtic gods, 94
Tinia, 63
Tiur, 63
Tlesnasa, Seianti Hanunia, tomb of, *50*
togas, 15–16, 50–51

tombs
Carthaginian, 115, 122–123, *123*, 130
Celtic, 97, 103–104
Etruscan, 48–49, *48, 50*, 59, *59*, 64, 67, *67*, 70
Roman, 28
Tophet, 127, *127*
torques, 86–87, *86*
Trajan, 21–22
Trajan Column, 22–23, *22*
Trojan War, 3
Troy, 3, 19, 108, 113
Tuchulcha, 64
tufa (volcanic stone), 14, 49
tunics, 15–16, 50–51
Tunis, 113
Turkey, 3, 6, 44, 75, 103, 108, 112
Tyrrhenian Sea, 2, 44

U

Uffington Castle, *78*
Ulster Cycle, 88–89
Uni, 49, 56, 63
Usil, 63

V

Valens, 6
Vandals, 7
Vanth, 64, *64*
vates, 95
Veii, 44, 63
Venus, 27

Vercingetorix, 76, *76*
Vespasian, 5
Vesta, 2, 27
vexillums, 34
Via Appia, *10*
Via Cassia, 46
Via Flaminia, 75
Virgil, 19, 21, 42, 108
virtus, 34
Vitruvius, 10, 19, 49
volcanoes, 24, 121
Volsinii (Orvieto), 59
Volterra, *46*
Vulcanus, 27

W

Wales, 74, 79, 88, 92, 95, 101
White Horse of Uffington, 90, *90*
White House, 8
wine, 39, 70, 77, 101, 103, 134, 136
woad plant, 99–100, *100*
wolf, 2, x
women
Carthaginian, 134–135
Celtic, 95, 97, 101–122
Etruscan, 67–68
Greek, 67
Roman, 35–36, 38

Z

Zeus, 63